WHY AND HOW
WOMEN WILL
ELECT THE NEXT
PRESIDENT

WHY AND HOW WOMEN WILL ELECT THE NEXT PRESIDENT

Eleanor Smeal

1817

HARPER & ROW, PUBLISHERS, New York

Cambridge, Philadelphia, San Francisco, London

Mexico City, São Paulo, Sydney

FIRST EDITION

Designer: C. Linda Dingler

Library of Congress Cataloging in Publication Data

Smeal, Eleanor.
    Why and how women will elect the next president.

    1. Women in politics—United States. 2. Women—Suffrage—United States. 3. Politi-
cal participation—United States. 4. Electioneering—United States. I. Title
HQ1236.S63 1984   320'.088'042   83–48386
ISBN 0–06–091109–03 (pbk.)

84 85 86 87 88 10 9 8 7 6 5 4 3 2 1

Contents

The Gender Gap:
What It Is and What It Means to You

You've seen it in countless newspaper headlines; you've heard about it on radio and television. Republicans alternately deny its existence or worriedly announce plan after plan for "closing" it. And Democrats, slow to recognize it as a political reality, are nevertheless counting on it to provide a windfall of votes for their party.

It's the gender gap—the measurable difference in the way women and men vote for candidates and in the way they view political issues. The "women's vote," a powerful new voting bloc, will make the difference in political contests. There is no doubt. The gender gap is the new wild card in political sweepstakes.

Women *will* elect the next president of the United States. We've already put governors in power in New York, Texas, and Michigan, and sent a dozen senators and Congress people to Washington. Remarkable victories—and not just for the officeholders.[1]

For women everywhere, these victories are a means to better salaries, more economic equity in divorce for homemakers, more job programs and training for single-parent families (usually headed by women), and a change in the spending priorities of our nation—goals that directly and personally affect each of us. These are just some of the issues the women's vote supports, and that support transcends party lines and political ideologies.

Until now, women have lacked the political bargaining power to affect public policy. Until now, our state and federal governments have literally been "of men, by men, and for men." Until now, the men who have dominated the political structure have not had to worry about being held accountable at the polls by women whose needs have not been adequately addressed. The result has been the enactment of legal and social decisions that worked against us, individually and as a group.

But today, women have a newfound power to elect the next president of the United States and to determine our country's political leadership and national agenda. The widespread perception of the gender gap offers a new tool for political power for American women and has the potential for being a catalyst for social change in 1984 and beyond. Where does this new political power come from? Here are the facts:

Women's voting strength, in sheer numbers, has been increasing steadily, so that women currently comprise approximately 53 percent of the voting-age population. Moreover, since the election of Lyndon Johnson, women have been casting more votes than men in national elections. In 1980, 55.6 million women and 49.3 million men were registered to vote and 6 million more women than men cast ballots in the general election. By 1982, 700,000 women, compared to 400,000 men, had been added to the voting rolls. Today a higher percentage of women than men are registered to vote (64.4 percent versus 63.7 percent). Since 1976, the percentage of women registered has been increasing while the percentage of men has been decreasing.[2]

Yet, ever since winning the suffrage amendment in 1920, women have been an invisible mass of voters.

Initially, the experts dismissed women voters as an unimportant part of the electorate. Their excuse was that women did not vote in such large numbers as men—a fact the experts were comfortable with, since it was entirely in keeping with their belief that politics was a man's world.

Even when women began to outnumber men in voting, the experts were quick to point out that a lower percentage of all potential women voters were registered. Their explanation, again, was that politics was "a man's world" and most women were simply not as interested in it. The experts also asserted that women voted as the men in their lives did—that is, men made the voting decisions, and women simply followed their lead.[3] With a sigh of relief, the experts went on ignoring any impact women were having in elections.

As a graduate student in political science in the 1960s, I became irritated by this dismissal of women in politics. The commonly accepted theory that women were apolitical and only voted as men told them was offensive. Moreover, the evidence for such theories was flimsy, based more on men's views of the political world than on hard facts.[4]

I long suspected that this portrayal of women was a myth. For me the myth was shattered as I began, in the late 1960s, my own study of women in politics and as I became increasingly active in the women's-rights movement.[5] For others, the elections of 1980 and 1982 shattered this narrow view of women and politics. These elections proved that women were registered and were voting in roughly the same percentages as men. Far more important, these elections showed that women could and *did* vote differently from their male counterparts. In fact, women voted differently from men across all age, race, income, job-status, and political-party lines.[6]

Today, all the experts agree that women and men have been voting differently since 1980 and that this difference has affected the outcome of many elections nationwide. *Indeed, women's votes were found to be the deciding factor for more political officeholders than men's votes.*

The *New York Times*'s analysis of the 1982 elections showed a male/female voting difference in 73 of 85 statewide races for governor and the U.S. Senate. The women's vote decided the winners of several closely contested governors' races in 1982, including Democrat Mario Cuomo in New York, Democrat Mark White in Texas, and Democrat Richard Blanchard in Michigan, three of the largest states.[7]

Today it is Ronald Reagan's gender gap that is attracting front-page attention, but in 1980 this gap was largely unnoticed. Reporters first dubbed it "Ronald Reagan's woman problem."[8] According to all the 1980 "exit polls" (public-opinion polls of voters who had just voted), about 8 percent fewer women than men voted for Reagan for president. Translated into voting power, this means that more than 3 million fewer women than men cast their votes for Reagan. In a close election, those women would have made the difference.

Since the 1980 elections, a consistent pattern has continued: Fewer women than men approve of Reagan's presidential performance. In July 1982, George Gallup polled a random sampling of Americans on Ronald Reagan's performance as president. The survey found 48 percent of the men approved of Reagan's record, but only 38 percent of the women approved. The gender gap was 10 percent. One year later, in July 1983, a subsequent Gallup survey found 51 percent of men and only 34 percent of women approving of Ronald Reagan's presidency—a 17-percent gender gap.[9] This gap has ranged from 8 percentage points to 19 points, usually hovering around the 10-point mark. If a 10-percent or greater gap between women and men persists, the Republicans are not likely to be in the White House after 1984.

The possible impact of the gender gap on electoral college votes also indicates why women will elect the next president. Remember: electoral votes, not popular votes, determine the outcome of the presidential race and each presidential campaign will keep a close watch on how the electoral votes add up.

Officially, there are 548 electoral college votes: each state's voting power equals the number of its U.S. Senate and House members; the District of Columbia has three votes. A majority of electoral college votes, 270, is necessary to elect the president and vice president.

During 1982, in three of the biggest states—New York, Michigan, and Texas (with 85 votes combined)—women's votes afforded the margin of difference. That year, gender gaps surfaced in winning campaigns in Massachusetts, Maryland, Ohio, Connecticut, and Arkansas, which could add another 50 votes to the list.

There are other political considerations that also contribute to this gender-gap formula for 1984. In five key southern states—North and South Carolina, Alabama, Mississippi, and Tennessee—Reagan won in 1980 by 1 percent of the votes. In all these states, women could cast the determining votes. In North and South Carolina, the statewide Senate races are likely to trigger a gender gap, since two of the most vocal opponents of women's rights, Jesse Helms and Strom Thurmond, are up for reelection. These five states have a total of 48 electoral college votes.

In Oregon, Minnesota, Indiana, Missouri, and Colorado, which should have strong female candidates running statewide on the Democratic ticket, a gender gap is likely to surface as well. The five total 46 additional votes.

Three of the largest electoral states—California with 47 votes, Illinois with 24, and Florida with 21—will be key in the 1984 presidential sweepstakes. Although Republicans won governors' races in California and Illinois in 1982, they did so by less than 1 percent of the votes cast. All three states have active women's-rights organizations, which will be registering women and coordinating extensive voting campaigns. Florida and Illinois were targeted ERA states in 1982, with big wins for women in state legislative races. If the margin of votes for 1982 is even a small indicator for 1984, the efforts of feminists in these key states will be critical.

Whether the impact of the gender gap is analyzed in terms of electoral college votes, it makes a compelling case for the conclusion: the women's vote will be the decisive factor in the 1984 presidential elections.

In 1984, there will be a major push for a woman vice president. Six Democratic presidential contenders—Walter Mondale, George McGovern, Senators Alan Cranston, John Glenn, Gary Hart, and Ernest Hollings—pledged before the 1983 National NOW Conference that they would seriously consider a woman as their vice presidential nominee. NOW resolved to work to strengthen the presidential ticket by advocating a woman for women's rights as the vice presidential nominee. Prominent Democratic women support the idea for 1984. Many are convinced that a woman on the presidential ticket would not only provide more political clout for women but also strengthen the ticket itself. They believe the time has come and are annoyed at the question "Is there a qualified woman?"

"Compared to whom?" says Ann Lewis, political director of the Democratic party. "Dianne Feinstein has already been mayor of San Francisco longer than Kevin White had been mayor of Boston when he was briefly the vice presidential nominee in 1972, and a lot longer than Sargent Shriver, who was nominated in 1972, but I don't remember any questions about their credentials. Congresswoman Patricia Schroeder has served in high federal office longer than Vice President George Bush. Every one of the Democratic women whose names are mentioned [Congresswomen Barbara Mikulski (MD), Geraldine Ferraro (NY), and Barbara Jordan (TX) and Michigan Lieutenant Governor Martha Griffiths] has a more distinguished record than Bill Miller [Barry Goldwater's running mate] and every one would make a better vice president than Spiro Agnew."

A woman on the ticket would work to activate the gender gap. Political consultant David Garth says: "Both parties should give serious consideration to naming a woman as their vice presidential candidate. There appears to be little hostility toward the idea of women in politics; indeed, there seems to be a good deal of sentiment that women are underrepresented—this should be a plus to women candidates at all levels. In every area of the country—and particularly in the West—there is a strong inclination to support women candidates for office, and the party that first taps the potential support for a female national candidate could reap important dividends, especially in a close election."[10] Garth's poll, done by Penn and Schoen, shows no real opposition to a woman vice president, but 18 percent of respondents were generally more likely to vote for women candidates, with an 11 percent gender gap—24 percent of the women, 13 percent of the men, being more likely. In a close election, these percentages could determine the winners.[11]

The message is clear: The 1984 elections—and all other presidential, statewide, and congressional races in the future—could be determined by the women's vote. As women's votes increasingly come to constitute the margin of difference, women's political power will continue to grow.

Why the Gender Gap Is Important to *Everyone*

A women's voting bloc for the purpose of political power alone is not the goal. What could be achieved by women's political empowerment is urgently needed—not only by women but by our nation. For too long women's views, which are different from men's on many issues, have been ignored to the detriment of women, the public issues they support, and, I believe, the greater good of our country.

What are these differences? Women's views on economic and social issues vary sharply with opinions held by men. Women are more intensely concerned with issues of women's equality, abortion, and child care. They favor increased social spending in such areas as education and the environment, and decreasing military spending. Both women and men abhor war, but women show more concern with its potential for devastation; they have a strong preference for negotiated settlements of disputes.

Even in areas close to home and on "pocketbook" issues, women and men differ. Women believe inflation is less under control and are more concerned with its effect on them as individuals. Both women and men are concerned about unemployment; but men think the government should stay out of the business of creating jobs, while women see a role for the government in expanding the job market and opening new opportunities. Women are more concerned about their personal finances and are very pessimistic about the future of the nation's economy. Men are more concerned about the nation's economy as a whole and are more optimistic about the future.

These are obviously generalities. Not all women think alike, any more than men do.[12] Nevertheless, all public-opinion surveys from the leading polling institutions have revealed gender gaps—differences in women's and men's attitudes about the major issues of our day. These differences are not particularly new, but only now have political observers and professionals begun to take serious notice of them.[13]

With the persistence of a gender gap, is it not conceivable that those issues women see as significant will finally get adequate attention?

This question doesn't stem from a new hope or a new idea. The dream of the suffragists, in fighting to win women's right to vote, was based on the conviction that their voting would make profound differences. From the first women's conference in 1848, when participants dared to express the then shocking notion that, as citizens of this country, women should be entitled to vote, until 1920, when the

Nineteenth Amendment was finally ratified, "the vote" gradually became a symbol to its passionate advocates of political power for women.[14] They dreamed of using it not only to protect themselves against injustice but as a tool for righting social wrongs. And the more they dreamed aloud, the more bitter the opposition became. The overwhelming fear of the opponents of woman suffrage—mostly men —was that women would indeed vote differently from men.

Although the gender gap did not materialize until two generations after suffrage, the hope of the suffragists that a women's vote would change our nation's priorities persists. A modern-day slogan in the current women's-rights movement expresses similar sentiments: "It will be a great day when our schools get all the money they need and the air force has to hold bake sales to buy a bomber."

American politics needs to recognize women's idealism, our views, values, and priorities. A sustained women's voting bloc and women's direct participation in the political process are steps toward such recognition. If you think the nation is headed on the wrong course, you can play a pivotal role in altering that direction by voting smarter, organizing, and making the gender gap count. Now is a particularly important moment to become politically aware.

Consider the fast rate of retreat that has occurred in three years of the Reagan administration in social programs of concern to women:

- Not only was the Equal Rights Amendment defeated, but federal programs to fight discrimination in jobs and education have been severely weakened.
- Federal budget cuts since 1980 reveal "inequalities of sacrifice," with programs that service women hit the hardest of all.
- Instead of eliminating inequities for women in the Social Security system—which result in women getting significantly fewer benefits than men receive—minimum benefits were eliminated for future recipients, 85 percent of whom are women.
- Federal appointments of women for the first time in history are at a lower percentage than that of the prior administration.
- The Supreme Court reaffirmed women's right to abortion, but reproductive rights—especially the decision on whether or not to terminate a pregnancy—are under constant attack by the Reagan administration. Substantial budget cuts in family-planning programs are an integral part of this attack.
- Record-breaking military spending has further enlarged the capabilities of the major nations to destroy the world in less time than it takes to read this book. Yet the budget continues to be cut

for urgent domestic programs that disproportionately affect women and their children, including disease inoculations, school lunch programs, and efforts to insure pregnant women's health care.

This list—which is far from comprehensive—grows every day. But the gender gap can bring about changes in many of these areas. As pollster Louis Harris has said, "The power that any group or any combination of voters can get is in direct proportion to the degree to which they are the margin of difference."[15] In 1980, women showed they could be the margin of difference; in 1982, women actually provided the margin of victory for several governors, senators, and representatives. In 1984, the gap may prove decisive.

A Gender-Gap Primer: Ten Points to Remember

1. Women can and do vote differently from men. This gender gap in voting appears among all subgroupings of men and women, and transcends differences in age, race, income, education, and party preference.
2. The gender gap is making the women's vote visible by providing a means of measuring it.
3. The gender gap is increasing the political clout of women, their political viewpoints and values.
4. Women represent enough votes to be the margin of difference— and provide the victory—for state legislative and congressional candidates, and will elect the next president of the United States.
5. The gender gap is widest when issues of concern to women are highly visible and polarized—especially when candidates publicly take opposite positions on issues of key interest to women.
6. By reaching out to women's interests, a candidate does not risk losing men's votes. Frequently when the gap has narrowed, it is because men have moved in the direction of women's positions on issues and candidates—which shows that women can and do lead in the political arena.
7. Consistently, fewer women than men support the Republican party in general and President Reagan in particular. For that matter, whenever Ronald Reagan's name appears in a polling question, a gender gap surfaces. Those Republicans with a strong record on women's rights often are not affected by the gender gap and have used their record to gain support from women.
8. More women than men presently vote Democratic. Currently, women comprise almost 60 percent of Democratic voters. An

analysis of University of Michigan 1982 election data revealed
that 50 percent of women identify themselves as Democrats and
only 23 percent as Republicans.
9. The gender gap is causing political leaders to have more interest
in women's views, concerns, and programs. It is already leading
to women's political appointments, especially in visible positions.
10. The causes of the gender gap are primarily the real differences in
the experiences of women and men. (These causes will be examined in Part II.)

The Origins of the Gender Gap

The key ingredients of political power are money and votes. Power
is also a matter of perception: Votes, to be noticed, must be attributa-
ble to an issue or to a constituency. In the past, women were not
perceived as a constituency that candidates needed to spend resources
to attract. No one could prove otherwise. After all, who could measure the women's vote? Unlike the Jewish vote, the black vote, or the
blue-collar vote, women lived and worked everywhere, and their voting patterns could not be analyzed by examining certain precincts.

Not until the media developed the election "exit polls" was it
possible to measure votes on the basis of sex. But for a women's voting
constituency to be noticed and attract widespread attention, an organized effort was also necessary.

Though some analysts now say a women's vote has been developing
for the past 15 years, no one noticed, much less measured it, until the
1980 election.[16] Even immediately before that election, when Carter
campaign polls were showing a measurable women's preference for
the president, polling and political-science experts were confidently
predicting that there would be "no discernible 'women's vote.' "[17]

Changing the perception—that there was no potential of a women's
voting bloc—was a critical strategy in the fight for the Equal Rights
Amendment. For that matter, the National Organization for Women
(NOW) aggressively pursued such a strategy, which resulted in recognition of women's voting power and the gender gap. Our determination to develop a women's voting bloc began with our experiences of
political powerlessness during the final two years of the ERA campaign. Briefly, here's how:

By 1980, the ERA campaign had employed most of the modern
techniques of citizen lobbying campaigns; yet we were still lacking a
handful of votes in just three states necessary for ratification. Clearly,

we needed a strategy to give women more direct political clout, a way to demonstrate to politicians in the 1980 elections—the last full elections before the 1982 ERA deadline—that they could not afford to ignore women as a constituency. If Democrats and Republicans would see that women's rights votes provided the margin of difference for victory or defeat, perhaps ERA could still pass.

Of course, there were doubters. Few believed that significant numbers of women could be organized for election victories on the basis of ERA. The conventional wisdom was that women and men were pro-ERA by roughly the same high support levels. But those of us who had spent the last decade working for women's rights issues knew better.

Public-opinion polls often do not measure intensity of opinion or correlate voting behavior with issue support. Certainly, a majority of men said they were for the ERA, but we knew who actually came day after day to do the work. Ninety percent of the ERA volunteers and activists were women. We believed our organizing efforts for ERA would affect proportionately more women's votes. This could be done only if ERA and women's rights were highly visible and salient in the elections.

By late June, and only two weeks before the 1980 Republican convention in Detroit, I was hesitant about organizing another major ERA action. We had just finished a rough campaign in Illinois, only to watch ERA miss passage by a few votes. We were tired and needed to regroup.

But during a phone conversation with Helen Milliken, a strong ERA supporter and the wife of the hosting Republican governor of Michigan, I became convinced that, late or not, we had to do it.

"Ellie, we can't just let them get away with dropping the ERA from the platform," she said. "We must have an ERA march. And I'll join you."

I put down the phone and within hours NOW's most experienced mass organizer, Alice Cohan, was on her way to Detroit to join local NOW activists, who within 12 days put together an ERA march of over 12,000 supporters. The march was so long that as we reached the convention hall, Helen Milliken and I and those in the front line could not see the end. Some speculated that the ERA march brought more people to Detroit than the Republican convention. Many of those marching with us were delegates and party luminaries from the convention itself. Media coverage of ERA activities at the convention was extensive. And within days the polls started to reflect that Reagan's opposition to the ERA and support of a constitutional amendment banning abortion was costing him votes, especially among moderate women.

Evans Witt, of the Associated Press, reported that about 25 percent of the public said the Republican position on ERA and abortion would make them less likely to support Reagan, with about 15 percent responding that these Republican planks would make them more likely to vote for the GOP candidate. On ERA, 6 percent more women (29 percent) than men (23 percent) said they were less likely to vote Republican.

Reagan's advisers—and the campaign itself—clearly did not show understanding of the intensity of women's support for the ERA. When Republicans dropped support of the amendment from their platform, GOP chairman Bill Brock said, "It's not going to cost Reagan votes either way." And Republican pollster Robert Teeter maintained, "ERA is not an intense enough issue with enough people to affect many votes."[18] Both were wrong.

We knew, however, that for our issues to have an impact on female voters in the 1980 elections, visibility was key. The Democratic convention gave us yet another opportunity to keep the ERA before the public and to remind political leaders that this issue was not going away. It also provided a way for us to show the stark differences between the Democrats and the New Right Republicans on women's-rights issues.

At the Democratic convention in August 1980, feminists organized to make even stronger the Democratic platform's plank supporting ERA and reproductive rights. After many all-night meetings and against incredible odds, we were successful. The delegates amended the already pro-ERA platform, denying Democratic National Committee resources to candidates opposed to the amendment. Moreover, another addition to the platform was a plank supporting Medicaid funding of abortions for poor women.

We lobbied hard for both resolutions, and suddenly found this effort easier than lobbying state legislators—because women held 50 percent of the delegate seats at the Democratic convention. Our past struggles to win equal representation of women at the convention had paid off. For the first time, we felt the direct power of women.

Throughout the 1980 presidential campaign, we called attention to Reagan's anti–women's rights position. From the conventions to Election Day, ERA picketers were at nearly every one of Reagan's campaign stops reminding women and the candidate of his opposition to equal rights. In what was perceived as a landslide victory, few people recognized that significantly fewer women than men voted for

Reagan. But we recognized it.[19] The December 1980 postelection issue of *NOW Times,* NOW's national newspaper, carried the story under a banner headline: "Women Vote Differently Than Men . . . Feminist Bloc Emerges in 1980 Elections."

We were buoyant with the knowledge that the gender gap, a women's voting bloc, had emerged in the elections of 1980.

By the summer of 1981, two ERA staff members, Molly Yard, NOW's senior political director, and her assistant, Betsy Dunn, drafted a booklet entitled *Women Can Make the Difference.* It included carefully compiled ERA polls as well as a chronological chart of what was then being called "Ronald Reagan's problem with women." These polling data were an impressive summary of most major public-opinion polls on Reagan by sex. The last column of the chart was labeled "Gender Gap" and showed the percentage difference in Reagan's approval rates between men and women.

Also included was an analysis of the 1980 elections, based on a *New York Times*/CBS poll, showing not only that 8 percent fewer women voted for Reagan, but also that pro-ERA women outnumbered anti-ERA women and accounted for a net *loss* of over 1 million votes for Reagan. The analysis logged Reagan's deteriorating position among women and included polls forecasting how women would vote in the 1982 congressional elections. As early as 1981, Harris polls showed women giving Democrats an 11-point margin, while men were supporting Republicans by 4 points for the congressional elections.

Washington Post columnist Judy Mann wrote about NOW's booklet and was the first reporter to use the term *gender gap.* As Mann pointed out, *"Women Can Make a Difference* was written to show Democrats who were still in power in key unratified ERA states that they had nothing to lose and everything to gain by ratifying the ERA. The opportunity was theirs to capture the women's vote—if Democrats gave genuine support to the issues on women's agenda."[20]

Throughout 1981–82, ERA campaign media director Kathy Bonk and I discussed NOW's findings again and again with the press. We regularly updated the gender gap information and provided it to reporters throughout the country. During this same period, we also supplied polling data to political leaders.

I had often wondered what anti-ERA legislators would say if we produced concrete evidence that their districts were overwhelmingly for the ERA. I did not have to wonder after the 1982 campaign. Extensive polls had been done on the ERA in key swing districts. Legislators looking at these polls, which they agreed reflected their districts' support for the amendment, still voted against the ERA. In one senatorial district in Florida, polls showed 74 percent of the constituents in favor of the amendment and 22 percent opposed. The legislator said he considered those numbers accurate but would still vote no, even if it cost him his seat. Actually it did, but I was sure at the time he did not believe it would.

At every step of the ERA fight, we felt women were regarded as politically expendable. The consensus seemed to be that after the ERA vote was over, "the ladies" would go away and "the old boys" could resume business as usual. To make it clear that "business" would never be "usual" again, we imprinted the slogan ERA Won't Go Away on bumper stickers, buttons, and banners.

We worked all through the summer and fall of 1982 in hundreds of elections under the battle cry "We'll remember each November!" In targeted unratified-state races, we had impressive victories. Record-breaking numbers of women filed for Florida legislative seats. Women more than doubled their numbers in the Florida Senate from four to nine, eight of whom were pro-ERA. In Illinois we also helped double the number of women in the Senate. In North Carolina, all four NOW-endorsed candidates for Congress won, while all five candidates endorsed by North Carolina's archfoe of women's rights, Republican Senator Jesse Helms, and his Congressional Club were defeated.

When the gender gap appeared in some 73 statewide races, we knew our work had helped to defeat many foes of women's rights and to increase the number of pro–women's rights officeholders. We knew how much anger and energy had been released by the ERA defeat into the 1982 elections. Our opponents were beginning to know also.

The gender gap, or the women's vote, was not strong enough in 1980 to pass the ERA, but it was a significant beginning. In 1982 it was more generally recognized and was key in winning immediate reintroduction of the ERA into Congress, with over half the members of Congress as sponsors. In 1984 and beyond, a decisive women's vote in elections can win equality for women.

What Is Causing the Gender Gap?

Those who predict that the gender gap will one day totally disappear miss the point. As long as women view public issues in a substantially different way than do men; as long as significant numbers of women are underpaid and discriminated against economically; as long as there continue to be more and more women who are economically independent of men—or, more important, believe they might be in the future; as long as more women live alone, or are responsible for their children economically; as long as such key feminist issues as abortion and the ERA, affirmative action in jobs and education, discrimination in insurance and in pay equity persist in the country without resolution—the *potential* for the gender gap will persist. Whether it occurs depends on the circumstances and issues of a particular campaign. This is why the gender gap appears to "blink on and blink off," to be present sometimes and disappear at others.

The important question therefore is: What and who will trigger the gender gap?

Right now, the triggering circumstances are many. The gender gap derives from the fact that women's circumstances are still so different from men's. Women are paid 59 cents for every $1 men make; homemakers are frequently without adequate financial security in case of divorce or widowhood; females are not only the more likely recipients of the government's social-service programs but traditionally are also the caretakers—the teachers, nurses, social workers. No wonder women view these budget cuts differently: We have been more dependent upon government services, from mass transportation to social security.

Pollsters and political observers are trying to analyze and dissect the various causes of the gender gap to determine which cause is the most important. First, many thought the main cause was war/peace issues.[21] By 1982, observers claimed economic issues as top factors causing the gender gap.[22] Usually, women's-rights issues are given short shrift as a principal cause of the gender gap.[23]

The quest for the most important cause of the gender gap, I believe, is a faulty pursuit. The many factors are not mutually exclusive, and in fact often overlap. At various times one factor may be more important than others. Yet each, or some combination thereof, has the potential of becoming an important factor in a particular political race.

The gender gap can occur because a candidate is insulting on women's-rights issues. Such a mistake can become a major electoral issue, as it did in the 1982 Michigan gubernatorial race. Defeated Republican candidate Richard Headlee was not only anti-ERA, he also mocked women who supported this and other women's issues. He once quipped that he apparently liked women more than his successful opponent, Governor James Blanchard, because he had more children. Blanchard treated women's issues seriously and chose Martha Griffiths as his running mate. The gender gap in this race was in excess of 8.5 percent (according to ABC and NBC exit polls) and Blanchard won by 6.8 percent of the vote.[24]

Yes, women have strong views on questions of war and the military, but if these matters are not relevant to a particular statewide or national campaign, they may remain just potential issues, while in other circumstances they could be very hot issues. If economic issues are highlighted in a campaign, views on them can be an important aspect of the gender gap. In fact, any combination or cluster of issues may activate the gender gap, depending on the times, the candidates, and the campaigns. Likewise, in a particular race the gender gap may not even materialize, because issues or circumstances did not actualize it.

The single thread that runs through all the issues that cause the gender gap is sex discrimination. Women view issues differently and have different interests from those of men because sex discrimination imposes upon them a differing set of experiences. For example, women view war differently than men in large measure because of their military exclusion and their socialization. Economic issues are perceived differently because women are paid less and historically suffer more from unemployment. And on it goes.

The irony is that while the gender gap is giving women more political power, some argue that women's issues have little to do with the gap. They seek instead to explain the gender gap by ignoring women and their concerns. Or to overcome the gender gap by appealing to yet more men. Or to take advantage of it by appealing to women without intending to serve them. The most obvious means of either narrowing or exploiting the gap, serving women's interests, eludes many.

Largely because the gender gap is not dependent on just one factor or cause, it will likely persist and intensify. And because the gender gap exists within all major demographic groupings (income, occupation, age, education, party, race, religion, etc.) of the population, its base of support seems secure. Within each demographic group, the size of the gap varies. For example, among Republicans, 74 percent of the men and only 62 percent of the women approve of Reagan's performance—a 12-percent gap.[25] Among blacks the corresponding percentages are a low 19 percent of the men and a very low 8 percent of the women—an 11 percent gap. Reagan's approval rating with high-school graduates, Democrats, and the poor is well below 50 percent, with a gender gap present but narrower than the 12 percent gap between Republican men and women. However, the size of the gap varies from poll to poll. A June 1983 New York Times/CBS Poll found a whopping 21-percent gap between Republican women and men.

For the gender gap to occur in voting, the differences between the candidates on the issues of concern to women must be widely known. Not only is this happening, it's happening more frequently now than ever before with the advent of the New Right and its current dominance of the Republican party. The marked differences between New Right candidates and their opponents frequently concern precisely those issues of greatest importance to women, and serve to intensify the gender gap.

I've written this book as a call to action. I hope it not only contributes to a better understanding of the women's vote but also shows what is at stake for women in this struggle we cannot afford to lose.

I

It's a Man's World Unless We Vote

Women's Rights
and the Gender Gap

After almost two decades of feminist effort, women's-rights issues are on the center stage of American domestic politics. Women support these issues with more intensity than men and have a better understanding of what is at stake.

With women's-rights issues under frontal attack by the New Right and the women's movement determined not to lose the gains of the past twenty years, women's-rights issues will remain key domestic political issues.

Because of what's at stake for women, because of the massive investment the organized women's movement has made in these issues, and because of the political calendar itself, I believe women's-rights issues will be important in the 1984 elections.

What is the impact of these issues on women's attitudes and votes? An understanding of the gender gap begins with an understanding of both the women's-rights issues and the movement that has placed them on center stage.

Political analysts often discount the importance of women's-rights issues in causing a gender gap in voting. A look at the numbers seems to show no great difference between women and men in their support of women's issues; by high percentages, both women and men support the drive for women's equality and its key issues, such as the Equal Rights Amendment. The apparent conclusion is that since there is no gender gap in support levels on these issues, they cannot account for the differences in voting behavior between men and women.

I disagree.[1]

One major difference—a major reason for the gap on these issues —is women's deeper level of commitment to women's-rights issues. More women than men believe sex discrimination exists, and they are more concerned with the problem. Furthermore, women are more likely to *act* on the basis of this commitment than are men. In-depth polling reflects this difference when the analysis penetrates below the surface of the "equal" support levels. Thus, while both men and women favor women's equality, women, when asked to rate the importance of the issue, give it a significantly higher rating.[2]

The importance of women's issues on the women's vote becomes clear once we look at women and men's voting patterns in terms of women's issues. An analysis of 1980 Reagan voters shows[3] that of those voters who favored the ERA, 49 percent of the men and 40 percent of the women voted for Reagan—a 9-percent gap. Furthermore, of the surveyed voters who recognized that women face sex discrimination, 58 percent of men and 49 percent of women voted for Reagan—again, a 9-percent gap.

The same pattern held true for abortion, although most people (66 percent) saw no difference between Carter and Reagan on this issue. Carter supported legalized abortion but was against Medicaid spending for it and often voiced his private opposition to abortion. Reagan is an active proponent of the Human Life Amendment, which if passed would ban all abortions. Men and women who felt closer to Reagan's position on abortion (13 percent) voted for him— no gender gap. Of the people who felt that Carter came closer to their stand on abortion, the men were *more* likely and women *less* likely to vote for Reagan (46 percent vs. 32 percent—a gender gap of 14 percent).

Election Day exit polls in 1980 showed that the ERA and abortion played a role in the voting attitudes and action of women. When CBS/*New York Times* asked voters what were the two top issues for them, 11 percent of the surveyed women and 5% of the men ranked ERA/abortion as being most important. In importance, this placed women's-rights issues right below the Iranian crisis (13 percent) and equal to income taxes (11 percent). The leading issues of the election were the economy, with inflation (41 percent) and unemployment (24 percent) ranking at the top. The fact remains, however, that on the ERA/abortion issues alone, Reagan lost about 1.5 million female voters.

Reagan's gender gap on women's rights has hurt the Republican party as well. Most Americans favor women's equality, and most men and women indicated that they felt closer to the Democrats' position on the issue. Women, however, were significantly closer to the Democrats than were men.[4]

This distancing from the Republicans, largely due to women's rights, cost the Republicans votes in 1982. An analysis of the House,

Senate, and governors' races reveals a sizable correlation between people's distance from the Republicans on sex equality and their votes for the Democrats. Again, however, this relationship was stronger for women.

Polling data collected during the 1982 congressional elections shows an even stronger voting pattern among females on women's rights issues. A comparison of three major women's-rights issues (ERA, abortion, and affirmative action) with other social issues shows that women are much more willing to vote on women's-rights issues than are men.[5]

There is every indication that this voting gap will continue into 1984. The majority (over 60 percent) of men and women believe that women face discrimination. In the summer of 1983, women were more likely than men to feel that they do not get equal pay (10-percent gap); that they have trouble getting credit (8-percent gap); and that they are discriminated against in promotions to executive positions (6-percent gap). The majority of Americans (85 percent) think it is important to strengthen women's rights in these areas, but women are more likely to say it is very important (an 8-percent gap). Most people (63 percent) see the ERA as a way of ensuring better job opportunities and equal pay for women. What's more, polls show that 10 percent more women than men are *extremely* displeased that the ERA did not pass in 1982.[6] In mid-1983, most women (63 percent) said they thought it would pass eventually, and 7 percent fewer women than men thought it would not pass (27 percent of women and 34 percent of men).[7]

Abortion and ERA still remain important issues for a sizable part of the public—both women and men—who say they would not vote for a candidate if he or she did not agree with their position. But more women make this strong voting statement on abortion (21 percent versus 33 percent—a 12-percent gap). The same is true for the ERA (17 percent versus 23 percent—a 6-percent gap).[8] The majority of those people who believe ERA and abortion are important voting issues are pro-ERA and pro-choice. In 1982, the women's-rights vote went strongly against the Republicans. The rejection is bound to be even stronger in 1984.

But polls are only one source of data for analyzing attitudes and political phenomena. If we ask ourselves, "Who really cares about increasing women's rights, women or men?" the answer is clear: Women and women's organizations are doing most of the work to eliminate sex discrimination and to keep the issues in the political arena.

Having spent more than twelve years fighting for women's equality, I do not need polls to tell me that women are more committed than men to equality. In recruiting both women and men into the campaigns for women's rights, I have found that the overwhelming majority of these recruits are women.

This should come as no surprise. It is women who are directly affected by sex discrimination, and thus it is women who care deeply enough to divert their lives to the long, hard effort to make the necessary changes in our society to eliminate discrimination. Many men support us, and some care a great deal, but they simply do not feel as intensely as women the pain, humiliation, frustration, and bitter disappointment of sex discrimination.

The behavior of individuals has been paralleled by that of groups and organizations. The drive for women's equality has involved most of the women's organizations of our country. Men's organizations may go on record in support of the ERA, but such support is not a central part of their activity. The Elks, Moose, Kiwanis, and junior chambers of commerce are not lobbying for women's rights in Congress, the state legislatures, or local councils. Some of these do not even admit women as members. Organizations with large male memberships, such as unions or church groups, may support these activities, but it is the women within them who are doing most of the work for equality.

I believe that without the existence of a major movement for women's rights, there would be *no* gender gap in voting.

In 1970, only a minority of women—40 percent—approved of the efforts of the women's-rights organizations, then in their infancy, to change and strengthen the status of women in the United States. By 1972 that support had grown to 48 percent, and by 1974 to a strong majority of 57 percent. By 1980, 64 percent of all American women supported these efforts, making it unmistakably a majority movement in this country.[9]

Feminists began the decade of the 1970s advocating "equal pay for equal work" and equal opportunity, pointing out existing patterns of discrimination, pressing for the enforcement of existing laws against sex discrimination, and winning passage of new laws. Women began opening doors and breaking down barriers. Throughout the 1970s the news media reported what seemed an endless series of "the first woman to . . ." stories.

In this drive, many new organizations were formed, not the least of which were the National Organization for Women, the National Women's Political Caucus, the Women's Equity Action League, and dozens of women's law projects and legal-defense funds. I could not do justice in just a few short pages to all the activities of the women's movement in this fast-paced decade,[10] but my own experiences at the local level may help make the impact of this drive for women's equality on women's attitudes and on the elections more understandable.

I was a local chapter president of the National Organization for Women in the suburbs of Pittsburgh, Pennsylvania, in the early seventies. During this period, we took legal cases to strike down sex discrimination against university faculty and female grocers, retail clerks, and plant assemblers. These lawsuits helped both working-class women and college-educated professionals, and in the process we all learned how the entrenched system of job discrimination really worked. We fought these cases and won, at least often enough to keep refueling our energy and commitment.

During this time, we also picketed and demonstrated, lobbied legislators, and worked with the media. Days turned into months; months into years. We became the veterans in the struggle and learned too quickly where the laws and guaranties were strong and where they were weak. The stubborn determination to add the Equal Rights Amendment to the U.S. Constitution was born in this struggle, for we had learned from hard-fought experiences that none of the existing laws was enough to guarantee women equal pay, equal job opportunities, or even a chance for an equal education, and certainly not "equality of rights under the law."

Loopholes, exceptions, sometimes the simple encultured prejudices of a presiding judge, employer, or government administrator thwarted our efforts time and again. The "two steps forward, one step back" phenomenon wearied some activists, but it angered and aroused many others. One of the fundamental reasons why the Equal Rights Amendment, which is a comprehensive tool to eliminate sex discrimination, will be a major election issue until it's ratified is the vast numbers of women who, at one time or another, have participated in trying to eradicate sex discrimination case by case, law by law. It doesn't work, and we know it.

In the final years of the Equal Rights Amendment campaign alone, millions of women directly and personally participated, by writing letters, lobbying legislators, making phone calls, marching in or attending rallies, going to fund-raising events, and contributing money they often could ill afford to give.

What's more, the ERA campaign has involved most of the major women's organizations of our country. These organizations and their leaders know through personal experience how important it is to ratify the amendment. They were the people who took on the lawsuits, lobbied for changes in Congress and state legislatures, and know how necessary it is to establish, once and for all, a constitutional guarantee for women.

A part of each woman is now *invested* in the struggle.

Thousands of women made great sacrifices for the ERA. They traveled to unratified states and reorganized their lives for the amendment. Prominent Americans also invested their time and energies. Betty Ford and Alan Alda co-chaired the ERA Countdown Campaign and both crisscrossed the country to talk to legislators and make public appearances. Political supporters and well-known public figures continuously helped to give visibility to the ERA drive, including Marlo Thomas, Frances and Norman Lear, Esther Rolle, Linda Lavin, Patty Duke and John Astin, and Sharon Percy Rockefeller, to name just a few. Millions of dollars and millions of hours were spent in the ERA campaign, and women are not prepared to write it all off as a "deductible loss."

Not knowing these women's experiences may turn out to be the Republican party's most serious political mistake. For example, in an effort to bridge the gender gap in the summer of 1983, President Reagan spoke at a meeting of the International Federation of Business and Professional Women's Clubs (BPW)—and made one of his best-known public-relations gaffes.

"And we have been doing a number of things here with regard to . . . recognition of women's place. I want you to know I've always recognized it," the president declared, clearly ready to charm the ladies with the ultimate compliment, "because I happen to be one who believes that if it wasn't for women, us men would still be walking around in skin suits and carrying clubs."

The reaction from the BPW delegates was a stony silence. Immediately after his speech, International President Polly Madenwald—a Republican from Oregon—criticized the president for the insensitivity of his remarks and went on to say that the Federation would not endorse any candidate who did not support the ERA. She urged the president to support ERA, the Economic Equity Act, and nondiscrimination in insurance legislation.

If the president's political advisers had done their homework, they would have known that the Business and Professional Women, one of the oldest women's organizations in America, with a largely Republican membership, had been one of the leading organizations in the fight for equal rights for women in this country. (In 1937, BPW became the second national organization to support the ERA.) The White House also would have learned that over the last dozen years the BPW had given at least $250,000 a year of its dues money to the campaign to ratify the Equal Rights Amendment. BPW lobbies on Capitol Hill for ratification of the ERA and for other women's-rights issues, such as the passage of the Economic Equity Act and the Nondiscrimination in Insurance Act.

During the late 1960s and 1970s, many new feminist organizations were formed for women's rights. They were reinforced by the emergence of a revitalized political activism among what were then regarded as "traditional" women's organizations. But these "traditional" women's organizations—such as the BPW, the American Association of University Women, and the League of Women Voters—though all founded much earlier, had come into existence in the wake of the suffrage movement. These older organizations, plus a host of women's professional and vocational organizations, unions with large female memberships, and church women's groups, became increasingly supportive of the women's-rights issues of the 1970s.

Meanwhile, more-radical women's organizations were formed on college campuses. An outgrowth of the peace movement of the late 1960s, they eventually helped influence the women's-rights movement to return to its antiwar and social-reform roots of nineteenth- and early twentieth century feminism.[11]

The network of women's organizations is big and diverse: young and old, pink-collar and professional, religious and irreverent, black and white, gay and straight, diverse in ethnic roots and class lines. But while there are often tactical disagreements within and among these groups, there is a remarkable consensus on the basic feminist goals of women's equality and the elimination of sex discrimination. The most unifying and politicizing force of the past decade has been the drive for strengthening the equal rights of women under the law.

Frequently, representatives of these groups meet in Washington, but their local counterparts also meet in cities and towns all over the country to discuss and coordinate their activities for the Equal Rights Amendment and various other pieces of legislation that further the advancement of women. These organizational women have a vested interest in the fight for equal rights and they are political activists, involved constantly in putting issues of women's status before the public. But the women who are active in these organizations do not stand alone; the vast majority of women support them.

The issues of economic equality for women will be salient in the

1984 elections because women's organizations will work to make them so. No public-relations initiative from the White House will persuade these women to ignore the Reagan administration's poor record on issues of economic equality for women. The congressional schedule itself will place key issues before the public, with the ERA likely to be on the floor of Congress for a vote right before the election.

The Equal Rights Amendment:
The Nonnegotiable Minimum

Only a short time after the ERA's deadline, the amendment is once again seriously being considered before Congress. Moreover, the public's two-to-one support for the amendment continues to grow.

The Equal Rights Amendment was reintroduced in Congress in January 1983, sponsored by a *majority* of both houses only weeks after the 1982 elections showing the largest gender gap voting in the history of our nation. Within weeks of the ERA's reintroduction, the amendment had some 245 *sponsors* in the House. Few bills are sponsored by a supermajority (218 constitutes a majority) of the House members, including its leaders.

Twenty-one additional women's-rights supporters were being sworn into Congress, and the Democratic leadership knew women had gone Democratic by 60 percent in the 1982 elections. Many of the new House members were there because of the gender gap.

Whether the ERA wins or loses in this session of Congress, it will be highly visible, and "no" votes are certain to haunt the predominantly male Congress in the elections.

If the ERA fails in Congress, it will be principally due to White House opposition and meager Republican support. With the Democratic congressional leadership embracing the new Equal Rights Amendment, and the president leading the opposition against it, we know the dynamics of this congressional campaign will be different from previous ones. The visibility of the issue and intensified efforts both on its behalf and against it will make it an inescapable part of the 1984 elections.[12]

If the ERA passes despite the opposition, many women will be inspired to redouble their efforts to change the political climate, not only nationally but in their home states, by defeating remaining anti-ERA opponents in their state legislatures so that it will have smooth sailing in the state ratification process. Thus, the political pressures generated will be greater than in any past ERA campaigns.

Why are we fighting so hard for the ERA? What is at stake? To answer, let's look at the complete text of the Equal Rights Amendment:

Section 1. Equality of rights under the law shall not be denied or abridged by the United States or by any State on account of sex.

Section 2. The Congress shall have the power to enforce, by appropriate legislation, the provisions of this article.

Section 3. This amendment shall take effect two years after the date of ratification.

The Equal Rights Amendment is a ban on sex discrimination in governmental action. And just as states are free to govern as they see fit within the guidelines of the basic principles of freedom of speech and religion, so, too, will the states retain their full powers to govern with the ERA a provision of the U.S. Constitution. However, within two years of ratification, how they govern must comply with the basic principle of not denying equality of rights under the law on the basis of sex.

An amendment to the Constitution providing equal rights for men and women is by far the most orderly and systematic way to achieve full equality in our country. The piecemeal approach to equal pay, equal education, and equal rights in general is not working. Some state and federal laws on job discrimination now contain loopholes that would be closed by the Equal Rights Amendment. For example, Congress has exempted itself from nearly all of the federal statutes prohibiting sex discrimination, as well as from the federal Equal Pay Act. State legislatures in a number of states followed the same path in exempting themselves from state antidiscrimination laws.[13]

In education, the laws are totally inadequate as well. For example, Title IX of the 1972 Education Amendments prohibits sex discrimination in educational institutions receiving federal funds; but under the current hostile administration, Title IX coverage is being narrowed and its effectiveness greatly diminished. The ERA would be a tool to stop such reversals and to provide a ban on sex discrimination in public education.

One of the most severe cases of sex bias in our laws is the Social Security system, whose inequalities condemn millions of elderly women to poverty in their retirement. Over the years, the more I learned about discrimination in Social Security, the more determined I became to pass the ERA. If the Equal Rights Amendment were to succeed only in reforming Social Security for women, the entire campaign for the amendment would have been worth it. The ERA would provide the constitutional mandate for systematic change to eliminate this form of discrimination. Reforming one small provision at a time at a snail's pace will not lessen the unfair and desperate plight of elderly women.

Of the 15 million women who were 65 or over in 1982, the average income was $5,300, compared to $9,100 for men. The average monthly Social Security benefit for women was $362, or about $4,346 per year. For men, the average benefit was $470, or $5,635 a year. For about 60 percent of older women, Social Security is the only source of income.

The combination of sex discrimination in life insurance, pensions, annuities, and Social Security results in elderly women being severely shortchanged. Millions of elderly women are falling right through the much publicized "safety net" into hopeless poverty.

Some critics say the ERA is just a symbol not needed to challenge discriminatory laws, and that Congress and the courts already have enough powers. Indeed, for women, the ERA has become a symbol —a symbol of equality of citizenship. But it is much more: By establishing once and for all the basic national standards for eliminating sex discrimination, the ERA would add constitutional impetus to updating the laws and to preventing women's-rights reversals now possible in a hostile political environment. The Equal Rights Amendment to the Constitution would empower women as full and equal citizens.

The ERA would put the weight of the Constitution behind existing anti–sex-discrimination regulations and statutes in both employment and education and would close the current loopholes, prompt state legislatures and Congress to repeal discriminatory laws and policies, and clearly guide the courts on how the laws covering sex discrimination should be enforced.

Without the ERA in the Constitution, women are a separate and secondary class of citizens who must fight for our rights law by law, state by state, and issue by issue. For this reason, the ERA is not negotiable and will remain a major public issue until ratified.

Abortion: Defending the Freedom to Choose

Three key factors will contribute to making reproductive rights a top issue in the 1984 elections.

First and foremost is the vast size of the female constituency for abortion. This group consists of women who have had abortions *and* those who want the freedom to choose.

Second, the drastic differences between the Republican and Democratic parties' positions on abortion will spark continuing controversy. The administration supports the Human Life Amendment to the Constitution, which would ban all abortions and also outlaw the IUD and some forms of birth-control pills. The major Democratic presidential candidates call for full reproductive rights as well as Medicaid funding for abortions.

Third, the next president will likely have the opportunity to make enough appointments to the Supreme Court to either secure or ban abortions (three pro-choice justices as well as two swing-vote justices on abortion are now *over* 74 years old).

Who will make consideration of these factors so important? The voters for whom abortion is a key issue. Women who give higher levels of support to legalized abortion include black females (82 percent) and those with less than a high school education. Never-married women and those divorced or separated also support abortion in greater numbers (72 percent), as do females in the West (75 percent) and Northeast (70 percent). The largest demographic differences among women are by area of residence. Suburban women and central-city dwellers support legal abortion by an 18-point margin above those females in the less populated rural or small towns (72–54 percent). Republican women support abortion over Democratic women by a 4-point margin (70–66 percent), with Independent women at a 72-percent support level.[14]

There is an increasing consensus supporting abortion and the availability of birth control. Seven out of every ten Americans believe the decision on whether a woman should have an abortion is best made by the patient and her doctor.[15] When *voters* are asked if abortion should remain legal, 80 percent say yes under all or certain circumstances.[16] Only a handful of people, about 10 percent, would make abortions illegal in all circumstances.[17]

The facts on abortion alone show how the issue has had a direct impact on the lives of millions of voters. Since 1970, about 10 million women have had legal abortions in the United States. Approximately 1.5 million abortions are performed each year.[18] The most recent figures from 1980 show that 3 out of 10 known pregnancies were terminated in that year by a legal abortion; a majority of these women were unmarried (80 percent), white (70 percent), and 20 years old or older (70 percent). Most abortions are performed in clinics (75 percent), nearly all of them during the first trimester (90 percent). The total number of deaths caused by abortions between 1972 and 1982 was 164. About one-third of these involved women with major preexisting medical conditions. Today, the risk of death from childbirth is about seven times greater than that from legal abortions.[19]

The hard facts on abortion, combined with the fact that millions of women use birth-control pills and intrauterine devices (IUDs), just begin to explain why so many American females of childbearing age have strong feelings about their political rights to abortion and birth control.

The message from women on reproductive rights is clear from both their attitudes and actions. Women want to limit the size of their families, and neither birth control nor abortion are options they will readily relinquish. Support levels for abortion and birth control are highest among women of childbearing age, especially single women and those with higher education levels.

Pollsters and political activists alike know that the tide of public opinion on abortion has turned. More registered voters are willing to cast ballots for candidates who support abortion rights and against those who propose to cut back or ban abortions.[20] As with the Equal Rights Amendment, a higher majority of these voters are women. And as with the ERA, women's intensified attitudes on abortion contribute to their willingness to vote on this issue and to the gender gap in general.

Most politicians indifferent to women's rights would prefer that the question of abortion just "go away." As Nanette Falkenberg of the National Abortion Rights Action League (NARAL) describes the situation: "A carefully orchestrated, dogged campaign by a small minority of people was used to chip away at legal abortions. They were successful in making abortion the kind of emotional issue that politicians dread. Just as our opponents raised the emotional profile of abortion in politics, we are teaching pro-choice legislators and candidates how to put the issue into a political perspective."

Throughout the country, women are organizing on this issue and making sure that voters know where the candidates stand on abortion rights. The real battle over these rights is moving to the 1984 elections, especially the presidential sweepstakes and the Senate races.

The message from a significant segment of America's female population is, I believe, twofold: Reagan's and the Republican party's positions on the ERA and abortion are intolerable and must change if these women are ever to support his candidacy and if the gender gap is ever to disappear.

The real difference between the campaigns of 1980 and 1984 is that more women are likely to know Reagan's position on reproductive rights. Reagan has publicly supported and worked for passage of the Human Life Amendment, and has supported an amendment to the Medicaid bills that prohibited funding abortions in cases of rape and incest. Even more telling is his article "Abortion and the Conscience of the Nation," published in the Spring 1983 issue of the *Human Life Review*. Here Reagan puts forward some of the New Right's most extreme arguments against abortion. By-lined articles are unusual for an incumbent president, and in this one Reagan equates abortion with slavery and claims that "we cannot survive as a free nation" with the continuation of legal abortion.

Reagan begins his polemic by misrepresenting the Supreme Court decision in *Roe* v. *Wade,* describing the decision as responsible for "our nationwide policy of abortion-on-demand through all nine months of pregnancy. . . ." He goes on to claim that "not a single state had such unrestricted abortion before the Supreme Court decreed it to be a national policy in 1973."

Both of these assertions are factually wrong. The Supreme Court, in its 1973 decision, ruled that during the first 12 weeks of pregnancy the abortion decision must be left to the woman and her doctor; during the second trimester (12 to 24 weeks), the state may regulate abortions in the interest of the woman; and during the final trimester, the state can regulate or prohibit abortions at the point at which the fetus is able to survive outside the womb, except when it is necessary to protect the life and health of the mother.

His second point poses a greater embarrassment. Before the Supreme Court ruled on *Roe* v. *Wade* in 1973, 17 states—including Reagan's home state of California—had either removed or revised their abortion laws. In fact, Reagan was governor at the time and signed the bill. Population centers, including New York State and Washington, D.C., already had laws similar to the current national policy on abortion before the Supreme Court spoke to the issue.

As with other women's-rights issues, Reagan revealed a shallow understanding of the facts and then took the most extreme *anti* position.

However, polls show that once voters know a candidate's position on abortion, they vote accordingly—and the polls indicate that 32 percent of the pro-choice voters and 30 percent of the abortion opponents are willing to cast ballots on this as a priority issue.[21] Since supporters outnumber opponents by a comfortable three-to-one margin, candidates have much more to lose if they oppose abortion and if their position is made known to voters.

For this reason Reagan's position calling for the prohibition of all abortions could have a crippling effect on a 1984 reelection bid. This is a particularly good prospect because women know that in 1984 they may be casting their votes not only for a president and other elected officials but also on whether abortions will be ruled legal by future Supreme Courts, given that the next president will probably appoint at least two new justices.

An additional factor contributing to the likelihood of abortion being a key issue in 1984 is the pro-choice position of the likely Democratic presidential nominee and the anti-choice position of the Republican New Right. Since one party's presidential candidate will probably be for women's individual reproductive rights and the other will be against that right, voters, especially women, will have a distinct choice.

The fact is, it is the Republican party that is leading the attack on reproductive rights. Prime sponsors of the Human Life Amendment in the U.S. Senate are *all* Republicans. In 1983, Republicans accounted for 70 percent of those senators voting for an amendment to the Constitution permitting state legislatures to ban abortions. And of the 16 committee chairmen in the Republican-controlled Senate, 10 have either cosponsored or voted for anti-abortion legislation. Although the leading pro-choice spokesperson in the Senate, Robert Packwood (OR), is a Republican, he is in the minority on his side of the aisle.

On abortion, as with the ERA, right-wing Republicans are leading the attack against women's rights. If Democrats become bold in support of women's freedom of choice, they could reap a windfall. But if they cloud the issue, as Carter did in 1980, they will depress the size of this potential gain. The GOP platform and the actions of its leaders do not reflect the sentiments of Republican party members on abortion. Republican and Independent women who support abortion choice, and are willing to vote on that issue, could in 1984 be the cutting edge of a Republican defeat.

Winning the Insurance Game

As NOW President Judy Goldsmith describes the issue to audiences across the United States, "Sex discrimination in insurance is one of the most open, blatant, legal forms of discrimination in this country." Women pay more than men for insurance—over the course of a lifetime, considerably more than an average woman's annual salary—and our return on this "investment" is less than men receive. What's going on here?

The insurance industry has almost challenged the women's movement to take them on. In 1981, Aetna Life and Casualty ran a full-page advertisement in several newspapers and periodicals, with the headline "Our Case for Sex Discrimination."

No major corporation would have run an ad proclaiming "Our Case for *Race* Discrimination." What motivated one of the largest insurance companies in the United States to publicize its support of industry practices that were negative to women, to its female policyholders, to consumers? The answer lies in the little-known but active lobbying campaign the insurance industry has waged to keep sex discrimination in state insurance codes.

I first saw the Aetna ad while in Oklahoma for the ERA. This ad, coupled with the highly visible Farm Bureau's massive lobbying efforts against the ERA in Oklahoma, finally triggered NOW's intense research effort on the insurance industry and the ERA.

What *was* the Farm Bureau, really (the name made it sound like a government agency), and why did it oppose the ERA? After all, we had considerable support for the ERA in rural America and among farm women.

Much to our surprise, we learned that the Farm Bureau owns or controls about 55 insurance companies.[22] In fact, the essence of the Farm Bureau was insurance. We already knew that insurance was a state-regulated industry. And from our experiences in many states over the decade-long ERA ratification campaign, we knew that the insurance lobbies, along with utility companies, were often the most powerful operations in the state legislatures. Our vote tallies on the ERA in the final four states disclosed again and again a noticeable and curious lack of support from those legislators with strong ties to insurance, either as agents themselves or as lawyers in firms representing substantial numbers of insurance companies. The ERA needed only a handful of votes and we were frustrated by the lack of movement in Oklahoma and Florida. If only we could crack the bloc of the insurance-connected legislators, we could still pass the amendment.

We organized a special insurance research team, which included Judy Goldsmith (who was then NOW's vice-president) and activist partners Patrick and Twiss Butler, who assembled all possible clues. This group analyzed facts and figures on policies and pricing, using the insurance industry's own materials and resources. At the same time, our political team surveyed voting patterns with an eye on the insurance ties. We also researched numerous state legislative debates on consumer-backed efforts to prohibit sex discrimination in state insurance laws.

A pattern quickly emerged: Many of the same legislators who were the standard-bearers for insurance companies in the unratified states were leading the charge against the ERA.

Dempsey Barron, the dean of the Florida Senate, is a preeminent case in point. Barron's law firm represented some 18 insurance companies, including Allstate, State Farm, and Nationwide. The senator is a member of the International Association of Insurance Counsel and the Association of Insurance Attorneys.[23]

Barron orchestrated the defeat of the ERA three times in the Florida Senate, twice by the narrow margin of only two votes. Everyone involved in the national ERA campaign knew Dempsey Barron's name and that he was one of the half-dozen men in the United States blocking the ERA. What most people weren't aware of were his strong ties to the insurance industry.

Nowhere was the insurance industry as powerful as in Florida (Jacksonville is one of the insurance capitals of the United States), and nowhere were state legislators as blatant in expressing their concerns about the effect of the ERA on insurance.

One senator, explaining to his constituents why he opposed the ERA, used insurance rates as one of his reasons. He wrote: "While I am for equal rights, I am against Section 2 of the ERA as it is now written which would grant the federal government open-ended power over the residents of Florida, and would strip Florida's women of the protections they now enjoy, such as insurance rates (auto/life) considerably lower than those paid by men."[24] Insurance was clearly on some of the legislators' minds when they voted on the ERA.

Once we understood the pattern of sex discrimination in insurance, the pieces of the puzzle fit together. The Equal Rights Amendment would provide a national ban on sex discrimination; yet the insurance industry, which in 1981 had assets of $700 billion, profits greatly from charging women and men different prices for the same product, and fought vigorously in each state against any legislation or legal actions requiring the same prices for men and women. The special interest that insurance companies had in the ERA was finally crystal-clear.

Above all, we learned precisely how sex discrimination works for insurance companies.

In auto rates, sex discrimination is similarly unjust to women and men. In all but four states—Hawaii, Massachusetts, Michigan, and North Carolina—male drivers under 25 are charged more than females for auto insurance, essentially because of the stereotype that "boys will be boys" and that they (as a class) are more reckless and fancy-free. After age 25, men and women pay the same rates.

Sex does not determine accident frequency. Factors such as low mileage, past traffic violations, and sobriety do. Women, on the average, drive fewer miles, have fewer traffic violations, and are more sober drivers than men. These factors account for most of the 30 percent difference in accident rates between men and women of all ages.[25] If rates were based on miles driven each year, past traffic violations, and sobriety—factors that an individual can control (unlike their gender)—women 25 and older would actually pay less than men for auto insurance, not the same, and certainly not more.

While the American Academy of Actuaries estimates that if equal rates for men and women were mandated, women as a group would have to pay $700 million more annually than they do now for auto insurance, this is scare propaganda that the facts simply do not support. Further, the actuaries who did the study were also vice presidents of Phoenix Mutual, Mutual of Omaha, and several other major insurance companies—hardly a disinterested or objective source.

Insurance companies claim to give women "a break" in life insurance, too. Based on the stereotype that women live longer than men, companies promote sales by highlighting the smaller premiums women pay during their lives as policyholders. In reality, the alleged "advantage" women get in life insurance evaporates under examination.

The industry charges more per $1,000 for smaller policies, which places women at a disadvantage since their lower income limits them to the smaller policies. The result is that we are paying nearly the same, not less, dollar for dollar, as men pay for a larger policy. (The average policy purchased by women is less than half the value of that purchased by men.) Also, many companies simply charge women *more* for life insurance. A 1983 GEICO mail solicitation listed rates for women aged 20–35 that were 9 percent higher than for men in the same age group.[26]

A number of arbitrary little industry "quirks" further reduce women's so-called edge in life insurance. For example, the non-smoker's discount, common to many policies, is significantly smaller for women.[27] And the nonsmoker's discount often exempts pipe and cigar smoking, an advantage not available to most women, whose smoking habits are generally limited to cigarettes.

The highly touted "break" for women in life insurance amounts to little more than a merchandising gimmick designed to attract more female buyers.

The illusory advantage for women in life insurance turns into a nightmare of financial insecurity when we look at the other side of the coin: pensions and annuities. Here women, who are at an economic disadvantage all their lives, are further punished as they enter old age, just for being female. Their monthly pension checks are smaller, though their costs of living are in no way reduced because of their sex (women over 65 pay the same as men for a loaf of bread). The different rates are based on the widely held assumption that women live longer than men.

What is the truth? While the insurance industry has not spread an outright lie, it has grossly inflated the reality and ignored a few important facts—one of which is that such factors as smoking and hereditary diseases have a greater bearing on the length of a person's life-span than does gender.[28]

Our study of women's life expectancy also revealed a little-reported fact: Of every 100 men and 100 women who reach age 65, 85 percent will die at about the same age. Thus, in retirement payments, *all* women are disadvantaged because 15 percent will live longer after 65, the relevant age when estimating insurance benefits.[29]

Elderly women are the victims of discriminatory insurance rates whether they are policyholders or beneficiaries of their husbands' plans. For many middle-class American couples, higher rates for men often mean they have to buy a smaller policy that provides lower benefits for survivors. In reality, only a small proportion of women are covered by either life insurance or pension plans.

Discrimination against the largest number of women occurs in the area of health and disability insurance. Companies charge women up to twice as much as men for the same coverage, and, to add insult to injury, usually exclude pregnancy benefits.[30] Again, the insurance companies play the numbers game, using statistics to try to justify sex discrimination. Some insurers look to the number of doctor visits as a reason to charge women more. However, our search of the data shows that females have shorter hospital stays and lose about the same number of working days as men, even when days lost because of childbirth are included.[31] Moreover, while companies claim group rates are nondiscriminatory on the basis of sex, employers who have more female employees will often pay a higher group rate.

Gender-based insurance rates cost a woman about $16,000 or more over her lifetime. Multiplied by millions of female policyholders, it becomes clear to us just how insurance companies profit from sex discrimination.

A strong case for eliminating gender-based rates can be made on the basis of social injustice. Insurance rates are no longer based on race or religion—such practices would be unacceptable even though data indicate that blacks have a shorter life-span and Mormons live longer. After the ERA fight, feminist leaders were determined to end insurance-industry sex discrimination, because if we did not, we knew the same opposition would surface in state legislatures again and again.

Polls show that people believe the ERA means women and men will receive equal treatment on insurance rates: 67 percent of men and 73 percent of women respond that equality in insurance is a likely effect of the ERA.[32] But most men and women do not yet know that females are discriminated against in the insurance rates they pay: Half of men and 43 percent of women do not, and a large number—17 percent— are unsure.[33]

The longer the insurance industry resists ending its discriminatory practices, the more the public will learn about its numbers games. Mary Gray, president of the Women's Equity Action League (WEAL) and a mathematician who has been in the forefront of this struggle, believes the industry is being irrational about its practices. "With some members of the industry," she said, "it's a matter of theology."

But the more exposure their "theology" gets, the less defensible it becomes.

In the 1984 elections, the leaders of the women's-rights movement will make insurance discrimination an issue. Numerous groups— including NOW, the Women's Equity Action League, the League of Women Voters, the Leadership Conference on Civil Rights, the National Federation of Business and Professional Women, the American Association of University Women, and the National Women's Political Caucus—are outspoken supporters of nondiscrimination in insurance. As with the ERA, ending insurance discrimination is high on the agenda.

The Women's Economic Equity Act before Congress includes the Nondiscrimination in Insurance Act. Members of Congress voting on this section face the powerful special interests of the insurance industry on one side and the gender gap on the other.

Child Care: Coping with
Inadequate Arrangements Daily

The Economic Equity Act's provisions for child care, unlike those for ending discrimination in insurance, fall far short of the need. Some provisions of the act, if passed, would increase the percentage of child-care costs allowed to be treated as tax-deductible business expenses. In addition, child-care tax credits could be refundable to those who file a short income tax form and do not take itemized deductions. The EEA also calls for funds for local community clearinghouses for information and referral services. All these proposals, however, still fall short of adequately addressing the need for accessible and affordable child care.

The absence of adequate child-care programs in America has reached crisis proportions. Experts estimate that because of the general unavailability of child care, some 7 million children under the age of 13 are left to fend for themselves; a shocking 1 million of these children are between the ages of 3 and 6 years.

Most employed parents are left to "cope" with child care as best they can. Baby-sitting by relatives, mostly older brothers and sisters, is the most common solution, but all types of arrangements exist. Some people rely on neighbors; some on family day-care homes where one woman, besides watching her own children, looks after several others for pay. Some hire individual baby-sitters; many others must rely on "latchkey" arrangements where children returning from school must fend for themselves and perhaps for younger siblings as well. Ideal arrangements are the rarity; coping is the rule. All this is a result of the fact that child care is a political hot potato.

I still vividly remember meeting a waitress who seemed particularly exhausted and at the end of her rope. I couldn't help asking her what was wrong, and she let the whole story pour out: She was on her own with two kids; her ex-husband didn't help; the older child was at a neighbor's and the younger one, who was sick, was at a friend's across town. She'd have to take a bus to pick up the sick child after work, and two buses to get home. Then she'd fix supper, and both children would need baths. And if the baby was still as sick, she could be up all night again. There was no one she could turn to for help.

Most employed mothers in modern-day America have had enough coping and juggling experiences to empathize with this account. And even full-time homemakers with children find that the picture is not all rosy. Many a mother who is lucky enough to be able to afford to quit her job after her child is born soon realizes she's just one adult and, no matter how hard she tries, she cannot be the whole world for her child.

I could afford to stay home full-time for our son, Tod (now in college). I prided myself on the fact that he did not go to nursery school—until the day after extensive tests at the University of Pittsburgh to determine why his speech was unintelligible.

"Nothing wrong with him, Mrs. Smeal. We recommend you enroll him in a nursery school—children learn best from their peers," I was told.

By the time I had my second child, I was a feminist activist and I helped found a nursery school. My daughter was in its first class. For years Lori had an easier time with school than her brother had, because of this head start. So did most of our nursery school's graduates.

Between the needs of employed parents and the needs of the children themselves, it is no wonder that quality child-care programs are filled to capacity, with long waiting lists.

Meanwhile, the same debate to which I succumbed 20 years ago continues. Should mothers work? Should women who work have children? Should child care be provided by the community or by private enterprise? What is "quality" child care?

The question of whether or not mothers should hold jobs is debated mostly among men—especially privileged men. A recent study showed that 66 percent of college men, compared to 52 percent of blue-collar men, believed employed mothers weaken the family. Most women support the idea of mothers holding jobs, with college-educated women supporting it the most strongly.[34]

A slight majority of employed Americans, both men and women, believe that women who want to hold paid jobs, rather than stay home to raise a family, should not have children in the first place. But here men tip the balance: 56 percent of men, compared to 43 percent of women, believe job-oriented women should not have children.[35]

Public-opinion polls on what people think is a woman's role as mother simply don't match up with Census Bureau reports of how people are actually living. I believe the reason the debate even continues is that adequate child care is not available, hence parents—especially those living the new and nontraditional reality—often are made to feel guilty. And the reason adequate child-care programs do not exist is because child care is a political issue that women have not had the clout to resolve.

Child care has been a political issue for some time because initially it was cast as a public service primarily for children of the poor. This ignored the widespread need for child care and reduced the constituency's size and clout with politicians.

The notion that child care is primarily a need of the poor has persisted over the years. President Lyndon Johnson launched the Head Start program as part of his "war on poverty." This program of child-care centers for the poor and working poor was immensely successful, but was virtually gutted by President Richard Nixon.

In 1971, then-senator Walter Mondale (D-MN) authorized a rudimentary but more comprehensive child-care bill and guided it through Congress. President Nixon vetoed it within days. In his veto message, Nixon described the bill as "the most radical piece of legislation to emerge from the Ninety-second Congress," adding that he believed such a program would foster a "communal approach to child rearing."

The theme of identifying child care with a "Communist" approach to child rearing has been repeatedly used by the New Right—which, by the way, is still attacking the concept of public education itself. Child-care centers also have been attacked as leading to the destruction of the family, rather than being recognized as a modern support system essential to it.

All the traditional forces against government spending for domestic social programs have been arrayed against child care. Opposition has come from the New Right, mostly Republicans, and from business interests either fearful of additional taxation or unwilling to share the existing federal dollar.

Meanwhile, early-childhood development centers, with after-school and vacation-time programs for school-age children, funded either by recipients on a sliding scale based on ability to pay or wholly by public funding, have long been advocated by feminist organizations. Feminists take the most comprehensive approach; others advocate such programs at least for the poor so that parents can work.

Whenever a new social program is proposed, especially one that benefits women or children, invariably the question is raised, "Where is the money coming from?"

Feminists answer, "The same place as money for the MX missile system."

Quality child care provides peace of mind for mothers, opportunity for children, and a vast number of jobs. Massive systems of destruction hardly lead to peace of mind, and they actually create fewer jobs.

I would argue that it is a matter of priorities: If women had more to say about the distribution of tax dollars, children and women would receive more and the military less.

For the past decade or so, the opponents of child-care programs have succeeded in blocking initiatives in the public arena. In 1979, Senator Alan Cranston tried to put forward a modest plan to stimulate the expansion and development of alternative child-care services: family, after-school, and work-based care. Again the Republicans and the New Right launched a frenzied attack and the effort was squashed in committee.

The need for child-care programs grows daily, however; and— despite the political opposition of the New Right—the climate of need and the gender gap have stimulated President Reagan and his administration to address the issue, albeit in a very limited way.

Several conditions now exist that will take the issue right into the presidential elections of 1984.

First and foremost, child care is a problem women face on a daily basis.

Second, while Republicans are trying to use their present child-care initiatives to bridge the gender gap, these are limited efforts that will point out the need for more comprehensive programs. For example, in his 1983 State of the Union address, Reagan promised that "a major effort will be focused on encouraging the expansion of private community child care." To date, action on this promise has consisted of a small campaign to encourage companies to help pay their employees' day-care expenses.

The private sector simply is not filling the need. Child-care chains that operate on a profit-making basis account for only about 6 percent of all facilities, and only about 100 on-site employer-sponsored child-care centers can be identified in the United States today. Other, smaller businesses and licensed child-care homes make up another 35 percent. A majority, 60 percent, are run by churches, Head Start, and individuals on a nonprofit basis. All of these facilities combined, public and private, fill about 10 percent of the child-care needs.[36]

The third reason child care could be a politically important issue is that two Democratic party hopefuls have authored child-care proposals, while the Republican platform and the New Right have fought all such proposals.

But women's-rights leaders know that without an outside organizing effort, increased support will never happen. Thus, the added spark for 1984 is coming from women's-rights activists themselves. Two days after I completed my term as NOW president, in December 1982, Elinor Guggenheimer insisted we meet in New York. She made an impassioned plea for help and assistance. She described our country's child-care crisis and told me she could no longer sit back and wait for someone else to get a major campaign under way. "The women of this country are desperate," she said.

I did not need to be convinced, nor do most mothers, when it comes to the issue of child care. We *are* desperate. And it is out of this desperation that action has emerged.

Ellie Guggenheimer has since brought together dozens of leaders in child advocacy, health and welfare, women's rights, the media, and Congress, under the umbrella of the Child Care Action Campaign. They are determined to raise public awareness of the problem so it can no longer be ignored.

Child care has long been thought to be just another "women's issue." Some argue that unless men become part of the fight and assume equal responsibilities in child rearing, the care of our nation's children will remain a low priority.

Indeed, men need to be involved in caring for our children. But the power of the gender gap can change the status of child care. I believe the outcome of the 1984 elections could alter the nation's priorities so that the question of adequate child care will be addressed.

Currently the various bills of the Economic Equity Act have been assigned to many different House and Senate committees. The major thrust for the EEA has been coming from Democrats and moderate Republicans: President Reagan, who said he wanted to advance women's rights statute by statute, has thus far not taken a stand on the EEA's meaningful sections. The lack of action on EEA from the White House and the Republican Right signals a troubling insincerity on women's rights.

The clusters of issues affecting the gender gap are not mutually exclusive, but interconnected. Women's-rights issues are only one part of what women must fight for politically. The economy, particularly the issues of inflation and unemployment, and the spending priorities established by the national budget contain distinct elements of sex discrimination with obvious links to the women's-rights cluster of issues, and it is these we examine in the next chapter. Though national economic problems have an impact on both women and men, the solutions offered by the Reagan administration have had a disparate impact on women. Women's-rights issues must be won if women are to achieve economic equity, but both basic rights and economic equity become unattainable if the problems of the national economy are placed on the backs of women.

Understanding the gender gap means also understanding the disparate and harsh impact on women of current economic policies.

Economic Survival
and the Gender Gap

Women's views concerning the economy, inflation, unemployment, and government spending differ significantly from men's. In the past, political analysts and politicians assumed that women voted their husbands' pocketbooks, or else simply voted according to the way the men in their lives viewed money issues. Women, it was assumed, did not understand these issues, nor were they interested in them. As a result, campaign messages concerning money, finances, taxes, the economy, and jobs were aimed at men.

Today, the evidence is overwhelming that women's own experiences with money are playing a major role in determining their views and votes. Analysis of polling data shows that, more than any other single set of issues, it was women's perceptions of the economy that contributed to the gender gap in the 1980 and 1982 elections. Women's concerns about the economy break down into three key areas: jobs, inflation, and government spending priorities. Each of these factors influences how women will vote in the coming elections.[1]

Though most people are not fully aware of the details of the national budget or economic policies, they do know that social cuts have been severe and that military spending and tax breaks for the wealthy have increased. The president has thus acquired an image of being unfair to the needy and overgenerous to the wealthy. This issue of fairness will also be an important one in the elections, especially with women. Women who already feel discriminated against in job opportunities feel even more cheated when they know they are sacrificing while others are not.

Women are more pessimistic about the future of the nation's economy: Men believe the economy will improve, women do not; the difference is usually a large gender gap of 10 percent or more.[2] Pollsters often ask a variation of the now famous question that candidate Reagan asked of the people in the Reagan-Carter debates: "Are you better off today than you were four years ago?" Many more women than men respond that they feel worse off; and the reverse is true—more men than women feel better off. Again, the gender gap on these questions is usually in excess of 10 percent. For example, in a 1983 Harris poll, 60 percent of the women responding said they and their families were worse off, while only 41 percent of the men felt this way —a gender gap of 19 percent. Conversely, only 32 percent of the women felt they and their families were better off, versus 53 percent of the men who felt this way.[3]

Women have generally disapproved quite decisively of President Reagan's handling of the economy, while men view it more favorably.[4] When specific problems such as unemployment and inflation are considered, women's and men's views also diverge sharply. Although both men and women have been concerned about inflation and unemployment, women are more worried and disapprove more strongly of Reagan's programs to deal with these problems.[5]

In general, women oppose Reagan's budget cuts, especially in areas of social programs, while men favor them.[6] The explanation frequently given for women's greater support of spending for social programs is that women are more compassionate than men. This, of course, is in keeping with the stereotype of women who as a class care more about the disadvantaged than do men. I have seen no data to substantiate this theory; public-opinion polls concerning presidential performance generally do not ask motivational questions. Yet politicians continue to act upon this theory, developing for public consumption a "compassion issue" or two. One aide explained that Reagan's issues have appealed more to men's concerns, which he explained by pointing out that "women don't understand interest rates as well as men."[7] The cure for this deficiency, he was certain, was in creating a feminine issue of compassion.

Stereotypes die hard. There are data to show that women's viewpoints on government economic policies correlate with their needs. Low-income women and single heads of households, for example, are the categories of people most in favor of these social programs.[8] Women statistically comprise the vast majority of the adults living in poverty. Professionally, women are the majority of the caretakers—e.g., the health-care workers, teachers, social workers, etc.—and as such we have a vested interest in these social programs because they provide us services and jobs.

Whether the motivation is compassion or enlightened self-interest, women are rejecting economic policies that adversely affect both them and the least fortunate.

National "Budgeteering"—Women Lose

Women have been the real losers in recent budget-cutting and spending exercises. The tax breaks have helped mostly the wealthy, while the spending cuts have punished the poor, mostly women, harshly.

In all the talk of budget cuts, it is easy to lose sight of some basic facts. The overall budget size is increasing dramatically, even in this day of much talk about budget cuts. Yet what is increasing is the largest portion of the budget, military spending; decreased spending is found mostly in the smallest portion of the budget—in the safety-net programs of social spending. Everyone is supposed to be sacrificing in these difficult economic times, but actually those at the bottom, mostly women, are being deprived of basic necessities while those at the top of the income scale, mostly men, are benefiting.

Where does the government get its money? About 45 percent comes from individual income taxes, 29 percent from social-insurance receipts, 9 percent from corporate income taxes, 9 percent from excise taxes (on gasoline, tobacco, etc.), 4 percent from borrowing, and 4 from miscellaneous sources.[9] In short, most of the money comes from personal federal income tax and Social Security taxes. With overall expenditures increasing while tax revenues have been cut, the end result has been the largest budget deficits in history.

Recent tax reductions have especially favored the wealthy taxpayers and corporations (in accordance with the theory of creating investment capital to lower interest rates and thereby increase production). The Women's Research and Education Institute's report for the Congressional Caucus for Women's Issues concludes: "For women, clustered at the bottom of the income scale, this [Reagan program] offers little relief. Female heads of households, in particular, will benefit little from tax cuts that accrue mainly to the highest-income taxpayers."[10]

The expenditure side of the "big picture" is somewhat harder to visualize, because it depends on how you categorize various items. National defense or military spending accounts for about 25 percent of the budget. If you include under this heading veterans' benefits, military assistance to other countries, and a portion of the interest on the national debt (the amount estimated acquired from financing previous wars and military spending), the national-defense percentage of the budget increases to about 37 percent. Social Security, unemployment compensation, federal employee retirement and disability, and Medicare account for another 33 percent of the budget. All other programs come from the remaining 30 percent of the budget. Social spending for the poor, education, nutrition, housing assistance, and the handicapped accounts for about 10 percent of the budget.[11]

To look at it another way, let's go back to the revenue side. Some 29 percent of the national budget comes from social-insurance receipts. These funds are assigned directly to such programs as Social Security, unemployment compensation, and Medicare. In other words, these programs are paid for from earmarked taxes. Initially, these trust funds were not considered a part of the national budget— and in that case, the military budget as a percentage of the total national budget becomes even larger.

Military spending has increased substantially faster than the rate of inflation in each of the Reagan annual budget programs. From 1980 to 1982, defense spending was increased some 50 percent. In proposed future budgets, the rate of defense-spending increases continues unchecked.

Military-spending increases mean a loss of jobs for both women and men. One study revealed that for every $1 billion of defense spending, women lose 9,500 jobs and men lose some 500 jobs.[12] Women, critical of the use of military spending (see next chapter), are financially injured by it disproportionately.

Social-spending programs in the period 1980–82 and projected into the future by proposed budgets have been either decreasing in absolute dollars or not keeping up with inflation. These decreases in spending injure women disproportionately but not exclusively. Women are the majority of recipients of these programs. For example, women-maintained households comprise 94 percent of all families receiving Aid to Families with Dependent Children (AFDC); 98 percent of all AFDC beneficiaries are women and children; and women account for two-thirds of all recipients of Supplemental Security Income (SSI), a welfare program that provides financial assistance to the aged, blind, and disabled.[13]

Spending cuts in social programs also reduce the number of jobs in teaching, health care, and social work, where women are the vast majority of the workers. With unemployment high, and financial need therefore higher, the cuts in these programs have been crippling.

Statistics are unavailable to determine how many families are affected by the cuts. Experts estimate hundreds of thousands. In 1981 an estimated 3.8 million families—11 million persons—were reported to have received AFDC. This year the federal program costs $8.5 billion, slightly over 1 percent of the federal budget.[14] In fiscal year 1982 and 1983, Reagan budget proposals requested massive cuts of over $2 billion in the AFDC program.[15]

About one-half of the working families who received AFDC in 1981 have been cut from the program. Another 40 percent have had their AFDC benefits reduced. Only 10 percent received unchanged or higher benefits. In addition, the Reagan proposals have introduced the concept of "workfare," which allows states to require recipients to perform unpaid work as a condition of receiving AFDC. Yet, under other sections of the budget, the funds for child care and job training for AFDC recipients have been drastically decreased.

Indeed, one of the hardest-hit areas has been education and training programs. With unemployment at record highs, women want a more activist government that would provide training and job opportunities. Instead, these cuts are producing the opposite effect. The overall budget category "Education, Training, Employment, and Social Services" was *reduced* 16 percent during the period 1980–82. Training and employment subgroupings within this category were cut by 55 percent. Education and training programs in other categories were also cut severely. For example, education and training of the health-care work force was cut by 46 percent.[16]

The Comprehensive Employment and Training Act (CETA) is being eliminated and replaced with a new program under the Job Training Partnership Act (JTPA). Both of these programs were to service recipients of Aid to Families with Dependent Children. JTPA has been funded at substantially lower levels (25 percent lower in the first year alone) and is shifting its emphasis to providing service in male-dominated areas. The other job-training program, the Work Incentive (WIN) program, which was to help AFDC recipients seek employment, is also being eliminated.

Drastic budget cuts to the poor and working poor are rife. Housing-assistance budget authority has been cut over the 1980–82 period by some 50 percent. Two-thirds of the nearly 3 million householders in federally assisted housing are women, and they are among the poorest four-fifths of all assisted householders.[17]

The Reagan budget works to cut "overlapping" benefits. Thus, the value of food stamps is counted in determining housing-assistance eligibility. What this means is that the poorest of the poor can choose between eating and shelter.

Neither has food and nutrition assistance kept up with inflation. The food-stamp program has been cut by some $2.5 billion in the past two years, with proposed cuts of $1 billion a year for the period 1984–86. More than 1 million people have been removed from the program. Not only was spending for school lunch programs reduced, but the special milk program and summer feeding program may be eliminated. Another food and health program that is in grave jeopardy is a small (less than $1 billion) but important program for women and children, the Special Supplemental Food Program for Women, Infants, and Children (WIC). WIC is a preventive health program that services over 2 million women and children and which experts estimate saves $3 in future hospitalization costs for every $1 spent.[18]

A favored method of the Reagan proposals for reducing social services has been the block grant. Under the banner of "New Federalism," Reagan policy has been to lump several programs together under one block grant to state and local governments. The local levels are to choose which programs to fund and at what levels, according to local need. The effect of block grants has been to eliminate programs for the needy. Typically, when several programs are put together under one block grant, the total federal funds for the block grant are reduced 25 percent.

The Supplemental Food Program for Women, Infants, and Children was placed in a block grant entitled Maternal and Child Health Services (MCHS), which also services blind and disabled children under 16, provides care and treatment for crippled children, and offers various "health services to reduce infant mortality and incidents of preventable disease and handicapping conditions among children." The MCHS funding was cut 23 percent. Furthermore, states are required to match the funds with $3 for every $4 spent by the federal government.[19] The states least able to pay are often those where the need is the greatest.

Block grants are also being used to curb family-planning services. The major federal program in this area, Title X, has been slashed as much as 24 percent in one year.[20] The minor programs have been placed in the Maternal and Child Health and Social Services block grants. The cuts are so massive in the area of family planning that they are undermining the whole program.

In the area of health in general, the recipients of both Medicare, a medical program for the elderly, and Medicaid, a medical program for the needy, have experienced cuts in benefits that will make it necessary for them to pay more of their own expenses, and many have lost their eligibility for Medicaid. This is a particularly difficult situation for elderly women, who on average are already spending about one-third of their income for health care.

The elderly have also suffered cuts in Social Security, and these cuts were particularly harsh for women. For example:

1. Elimination of the minimum benefit for new beneficiaries—85 percent of whom are females.
2. Phase-out of post–secondary-school benefits.
3. Phase-out of survivors' benefits when youngest child reaches 16 years—particularly difficult for widows.[21]

Unemployment from Women's Perspective

During periods of unemployment, two events occur simultaneously: People lose their jobs, and they are often forced to take much lower-paying work. During the recent period of unemployment, women have not only lost jobs but when they have been "lucky" enough to find other work, it has been at lower wages in dead-end positions. Essentially, the gains of affirmative action in placing women in nontraditional, higher-paying jobs are being lost. Thus, although both women and men worry about unemployment, women consistently show higher levels of concern about it and are more critical of Reagan's handling of the problem.

During 1982 and the first six months of 1983, women experienced slightly lower unemployment rates than men: In 1982, women's unemployment rate was 9.4 percent while men's was 9.9 percent. But an examination of unemployment figures over the past decade shows that in every year except 1982 women have experienced higher unemployment rates: For the decade 1972–82, men's average rate was 6.2 percent while women's was 7.5 percent.[22]

A closer look at unemployment shows how some women are hit twice as hard as men, especially those women who are already economically disadvantaged. In 1982, married men had the lowest unemployment rate of all Americans—6.5 percent, compared to married women at 7.4 percent. Women who maintain families alone experienced jobless rates of 11.7 percent, compared to 9.8 percent for similarly situated men. But the hardest-hit were those workers with unemployed spouses, who themselves suffered rates of unemployment at 18.1 percent for men and 20.7 percent for women.[23]

Blacks experienced unemployment rates almost twice as high as whites' (17.3 percent versus 8.6 percent) in 1982. Unemployment rates for teen-agers are the highest of any grouping: 23 percent for white males, 22 percent for white females, 47 percent for black males, and 49 percent for black females.[24]

In certain job categories, women are hurt harder by unemployment. In blue-collar jobs, for example, women's jobless rates were at 16.4 percent, compared to 13.7 percent for men. These rates also show that women in nontraditional, blue-collar jobs are suffering much higher rates than women in other categories—such as professionals at 3 percent, clericals at 7 percent, and service workers at 10 percent.[25] Many of these females will never return to their higher-paying blue-collar jobs.

Women and minorities know only too well the meaning of the slogan Last Hired, First Fired. When there is a shortage of jobs, they will suffer disproportionately with not only higher unemployment rates, but fewer opportunities, lower pay, and limited promotions.

Thus, more women than men believe government should play a more active role in creating jobs.[26] Blacks feel stronger about this than whites, with black women's support the highest. While both men and women favor the passage of a full-employment bill, women do so by a wider margin. Of those women and men who disapprove of Reagan's performance and are concerned with unemployment, women voters who are divorced, separated, or single are significantly more concerned about job losses.[27]

Women fear being pushed out of the paid labor force to "solve" the nation's unemployment problem, as was the case in the 1930s and late 1940s. I can still recall the bitterness of an aunt who was "laid off" from a high-paying factory job after World War II veterans returned. She never again held a job that paid as well.

A significantly smaller percentage of women than men are in union jobs. Only 23 percent of the labor force is unionized, and only 30 percent of these are women. Therefore their work not only is lower paying but frequently does not have decent "fringe benefits"—health insurance, paid vacation, etc. As Congresswoman Barbara Mikulski (D-MD) has said, "For women, who are unprotected by unions, government must be their collective-bargaining agent for job opportunities, benefits, and pensions."

Women are increasingly turning to government to defend their rights, create job opportunities, and eliminate job and wage discrimination. Men still have faith in the Horatio Alger stories of making it the hard way, "pulling yourself up by your own bootstraps." Women are far more skeptical. Although there still are women who feel that hard work pays off, almost half of the women do not think so. The lack of decent-paying jobs for women is a large part of this pessimism.

Inflation from Women's Perspective

Why do women view inflation as one of the most crucial political issues? And why, even as the inflation rate has been decreasing, does the gender gap grow?

First, women do not see the prices of consumer items decreasing. And second, women do not feel better off as the economy "turns the corner." Women do not think they can put more money into savings; in fact, more women than men feel just the opposite—that they can save less money now.[28]

We have lived in inflationary times since World War II. Today, when the rate of inflation is said to be going down, this means only a decrease in the rate of price increases. Prices are still rising, and they are rising from the very high recent inflation rates of the period 1979–81. Women, who do most of the family purchasing, know prices. The newspaper headlines may say inflation is down, but when we buy the groceries, shoes, and clothing, we realize prices are up and climbing.

Since the average woman is paid less and is often supporting herself and a family on her income, these high prices seem all the more outrageous. Moreover, during inflation, wages increase as a percentage of a person's existing pay, and 5 percent of a $10,000 annual salary is a considerably smaller pay raise than 5 percent of a $20,000 salary. Throughout the inflationary period, women wage earners' purchasing power has thus been decreasing at a faster rate than men's. And there has been no catch-up period.

Economic Issues, Women and the 1984 Elections

In 1984, political candidates who address women's economic plight will benefit. Candidates who speak about smokestack industries without referring to service industries, which employ more women, will risk losing female voters. Candidates determined to tell women that they have never had it so good will not be believed.

Moreover, women's views, experiences, and vested interests are counter to the current conservative trends in economics. Women want and need an activist government that creates enough jobs to expand opportunities. Conservatives have tended to oppose government job programs in general, let alone those that would create jobs for women as well as for men.

Reagan has repeatedly opposed government job-creation programs, and conservative proposals to solve unemployment always have a heavy dosage of help for the employer, not the unemployed. For example, to solve teen-age unemployment, the administration proposed a subminimum wage, $2.50 per hour, for teen-agers—some 25 percent lower than the current minimum wage of $3.35 an hour. The subminimum wage is a favorite proposal of conservatives and is adamantly opposed by labor unions. The unions are fighting the creation of a cheap labor pool that they fear will lead to teen-agers replacing their parents at work with lower wages.

Meanwhile, Democrats are pushing for jobs bills, albeit mostly for men's jobs. Congress continues to save employment and training programs slated for extinction by the administration. Democratic leaders in Congress continue to fight for bills creating new jobs. The few women in Congress led the fight to amend the small 1983 jobs bill to include funds for jobs in the social-services sector, which is composed primarily of female workers. Prior to this, jobs bills have focused on industries employing primarily men.

Jobs and budget spending will be an election issue for women's organizations. Women's professional and labor groups—such as teachers, social workers, and nurses—are organizing for the elections against politicians who support cutting social spending. For women's organizations, be they representative of employed women or not, economic issues are becoming increasingly important in electoral targeting. The cuts in programs have been so extensive that women's organizations that previously supported candidates based on their women's-rights votes are now including the candidates' actions or views on budget spending. The current conservative domination of the budgeting process and the extremism of the Reagan proposals have mandated this change.

When the statistics are reviewed on women's attitudes and economic plight, it becomes clear that more and more women are developing attitudes of the have-nots toward government. Traditionally, people economically deprived have looked to government for services and opportunities, and for representation of their interests. More and more women, either completely dependent or increasingly dependent

upon their own earning power, or believing they might be in the
future, want government to even the stakes in what has been so far
an unequal, unfair, and economically crippling game for them and
their families.

War, Violence,
and the Gender Gap

For women, war and the military are of pivotal concern today. Nuclear devastation threatens our world. Increased defense spending has gutted social programs—programs that employ mostly women and provide services to millions of families. Nowhere have women been more excluded from decision-making than in military and foreign affairs. What are the ramifications of women's exclusion and the differences between women and men on these issues? How do they affect the gender gap?

Since World War II, women and men have been more deeply divided on the issue of war than on any other single issue.[1] To be sure, in answer to the pollsters' question of whether people want war or peace, everyone—male and female—says they want peace, just as a nuclear freeze has high levels of support from all Americans. But women are more consistently troubled than men when asked how they feel about the possibility of war and of heightened defense spending.

These differences begin, as do many, in the stereotypes of child's play: Johnny plays soldier; Suzy can be the nurse, or she can just go away and play house. The message remains the same in adulthood: War is a man's game; women can be nurses or victims, soldiers' wives or soldiers' widows. They can even be called upon to be "the woman behind the man behind the gun," as one World War II poster declared. But with a few rare exceptions (like Margaret Thatcher and Indira Gandhi), it is men, and men only, who decide when the "game" begins and ends.

A strong majority of women see war as an outmoded way of settling differences. Men, on the other hand, are split on the subject, with a plurality seeing war as "sometimes necessary."[2]

What does this situation mean for future elections? In 1984 and beyond, it will mean a great deal. A strong majority of women (57–39 percent) have been worried that Reagan will involve the United States in war, while a substantial majority of men (56–41 percent) are not concerned—a 16-point gap.[3] Consistently, women have been concerned about Ronald Reagan's warmongering image. He has publicly conjectured about the feasibility of "winning" a limited nuclear exchange with the Soviet Union—which he envisioned taking place in Europe, to the outrage of the civilian population there.

Women also strongly oppose federal spending to develop various weapon systems: A majority of women oppose the MX missile, while men have been evenly divided on it.[4] At stake here are billions upon billions of dollars that have been consumed by the production of military arsenals. Fortunately, many weapon systems become obsolete without ever having been used. Unfortunately, however, obsolescence becomes an urgent signal to spend additional billions on developing replacements. The constant escalation of the arms race continues, with intense advocacy of one weapon system over another, and with an almost casual objectivity in calculating casualties in "mega-" terms. Stockpiling of instruments of destruction has left us with the capacity to annihilate all human life and the planet itself, not just once but several times.

The gender gap turns into a gender gulf on these issues of war and increased defense spending. These political responses are deeply rooted in the traditional exclusion of women from the military and from consideration of military matters. Most men have been prepared mentally for the possibility of serving in the armed forces, and millions have served. Frequently, men who have served, and even those who have not, feel that they, not women, are put at risk in war. This risk, many men believe, entitles them to certain rights, including exclusive decision-making on issues of war and foreign affairs.[5] Moreover, many men believe that because of their training, only they understand these matters.

As a result, women again and again are excluded from military and foreign-policy decisions. For example, the Scowcroft Commission, which developed policy on the MX missile system, had no female members, although female opinions on the MX were significantly different from those of men. Likewise, Reagan appointed an all-male commission on Central America, headed by Henry Kissinger. He justified the lack of females by claiming the administration had done "so much" in "appointing women that we're no longer seeking a token or something."

Traditionally excluded from the "warrior" class, women have felt an increasing disdain for war. We know that everyone is at risk in modern warfare. We do not need to pretend to understand war. We see no glorification or possible rite of "manhood" through it. And we are increasingly worried about the potential for total destruction. Men, thinking they understand war, are not as fearful of its potential. When the Gallup survey asked people their feelings about the likelihood of nuclear war in the next ten years, a majority of women said they thought it was likely, while a larger majority of men felt the opposite—that nuclear war was unlikely. The gap on the likelihood was 10 percent.[6]

It should come as no surprise that women's attitudes toward sending troops to war also have differed sharply from men's. This difference could be seen years ago in attitudes toward the Korean War: About half of the men (48 percent) but less than a third of the women (32 percent) thought we should have become involved, a 16-percent gap. And almost from the outset of the Vietnam War, women were more opposed to United States involvement than men: More than two-thirds of the women as compared to slightly more than half of the men thought the Vietnam War was a mistake—a 16-percent gap.[7]

This pattern is, if anything, more pronounced today. When asked the question "If it was clear that El Salvador was going to be taken over by Communist forces, would you favor or oppose sending troops to fight to prevent a Communist take-over?" men say yes, send troops, while women, by 11 points, oppose sending troops—a 13-percent gap on sending troops.[8]

Economic Hardships of Women's Exclusion from the Military

As much as most women abhor war, when women have been needed by the military, we have responded. When women have no longer been needed to "man" the factories at home or to fill military recruitment shortfalls, we have been turned away. We have been treated as an elastic part of the military's labor force, without the benefits accorded our male counterparts.

Women are excluded by the military in two ways: First, their total numbers in all branches are limited by small recruitment quotas; and, second, once in the military, women are barred from numerous job categories. The rationale for both of these limitations is based on the fact that women are excluded by statute, policies, and regulations from serving in combat.

The closing of military jobs to women has dire economic consequences for women both inside and outside the military sector, espe-

cially with a runaway military budget. Denying women access to
nearly all the available military jobs and to the extensive training and
employment benefits offered by the largest employer in America is a
significant factor in keeping women in low-level, low-paying jobs in
the civilian work force. Furthermore, the preferential hiring of veterans for federal, state, and local government civilian jobs keeps highly
qualified women out of better-paying positions, in some cases for their
entire lives.

Is the no-combat rule a valid reason for excluding women from
most military jobs? At first this rule appears logical to many; but, like
most forms of sex discrimination, closer examination reveals it to be
an arbitrary means of penalizing women economically. Excluding
women from combat does not protect us; it hurts us, particularly
because the no-combat-for-women issue is a phony one. The definition
of *combat* is altered time and again to suit the convenience of the
military.

Women who work with the military establishment, from Demo-
cratic Congresswoman Patricia Schroeder, a member of the House
Armed Services Committee for ten years, to Retired Major General
Jeanne Holm, a Republican who served in President Ford's White
House, describe the meaning of combat as anything the military wants
it to be at any given time.

Ironically, women have always served in combat zones. During
World War II, 350,000 women held military jobs, ranging from me-
chanics to typists, from parachute riggers and radio operators to
airplane ferry pilots. But *technically* women have been and remain
banned from combat-designated jobs even though females have served
in combat roles and will see combat again if another "shooting war"
breaks out.

The debate over whether women should be in combat and the image
of women in foxholes, so often evoked by those who oppose women's
rights, has served to distort the real issue of equal rights for women
inside and outside the military. The combat issue has become a smoke
screen for obscuring the fact that women in the military have been
cheated out of equal pay and full educational opportunities. More
important, this exclusion has diminished the potential voice of women
in foreign and military affairs. If there are future wars, women will
be in them, but will be denied the benefits and advances granted their
male counterparts. As former undersecretary of the air force Antonia
Chayes described the problem to Congress: "In any future wars, I
have no doubt women will face more severe risks of injury, just as U.S.
civilians will. What we achieve by barring women from combat roles

is an obstacle to career advances, and little enhancement of protections."[9]

The combat rationale is weakest when considered in terms of the conditions of modern warfare, where there are no "front lines," where the combat zone can be the whole country, indeed the whole hemisphere. Is it more dangerous to be in a tanker plane—a noncombat classification in which women are allowed to serve—or in a fighter plane, a combat classification, from which they are excluded? Ironically, tanker planes, which fuel fighters, are often the first target of the enemy and are therefore much more hazardous.

I always thought that *combat* implied open hostilities—that combat was "where the bullets fly." Actually, combat jobs are most often defined by what the task is. Women can be assigned to combat zones as nurses, yet not be in a combat-designated job. Thus women have the risk without the commensurate pay or benefits.

Why the artificial definitions? Not to protect women but to save the military money. Keeping women's numbers down artificially through combat restrictions means the numbers of females in the military remain small. If quotas limiting the number of women were lifted and opportunities were made equal to men's, women would start to flood into the military from their low-paying civilian jobs. The Department of Defense keeps its own payrolls small by underpaying women in the civilian sector. The work women do as civilian employees of the Department of Defense would command higher wages if they were doing it as military personnel.

These economic inequalities have served the military budget in other ways, too. Women's representation in the military has expanded or shrunk in the past ten years in remarkable coincidence with unemployment statistics. When unemployment has dropped to low levels and recruitment for the All-Volunteer Armed Forces has been difficult, the regulations restricting women's numbers have been relaxed. When unemployment has grown, these regulations have become tougher and the number of women in the military has decreased.

This Yo-Yo effect was particularly obvious in 1973, when the draft ended and the all-volunteer service suddenly encountered trouble. At that time, due to military quota ceilings on female recruits, women constituted about 1.6 percent of the army, navy, air force, marines, and coast guard combined.[10] By the mid-1970s, the quota ceiling was lifted, and women helped to fill the shortfalls in volunteer recruits. Concurrently, women were being admitted for the first time to officer-training schools, including West Point, Annapolis, and the Air Force Academy. Still, the combat restrictions remained, limiting women's climb on the career ladder.

The Pentagon subsequently revised its job descriptions and re-defined *combat*. The military opened more occupations for women, hoping this would encourage more females to enlist. Their strategy worked. By 1980, about 170,000 women (8.4 percent of the total force) were serving in the five major branches.[11]

Although women have been limited in military work, their work is not second-class; performance tests have confirmed their high quality as soldiers. During the Carter administration, extensive testing was done to find out what effects an integrated military was having on troop morale, performance, and military readiness. It was learned that integrated troops with both women and men performed as well as or better than the male-only or female-only squads. Moreover, women had considerably lower rates of absence without leave, desertion, alcoholism, and drug abuse,[12] and thus were less likely to present discipline problems and lost less time on the job. Perhaps their excep-tional performance has to do with the fact that the standards for women in the military are much higher than for men. For example, in the army, navy, and marines, women are required to have a high-school diploma. Men are not.[13]

The overall effect of the discriminatory practices has been that the average female recruit is much smarter and better educated than the average male. Since the best indicators of potential success in the military are educational level and reading ability (according to the Department of Defense),[14] the female recruit is more than equal. One ironic fact that proves their abilities: In some sections of the military, women train for combat jobs that they are prohibited from filling.[15]

Today, the small gains women made in the 1970s are gradually being reversed. As in all other areas of equal rights, the Reagan administration began soon after Inauguration Day in 1981 to move women backward in the military. In February 1981, before the Senate Armed Services Subcommittee on Manpower and Personnel, an offi-cial from the Department of Defense told Congress the army was reevaluating President Carter's plan to increase the number of women in the armed forces.[16]

The Reagan administration began a series of studies to determine whether women's increased role in the military had affected combat readiness. The next phase came in June 1981, when the army chief of staff announced, "I have called a pause to further increases in the numbers of army women."[17] And finally, the Department of Defense announced in 1982 that the army was closing an additional 23 career fields to women because it had changed the *combat* definitions.[18]

Women had already been performing these jobs for years. Now, through no fault of their own, they were being robbed of them, and of the possibility of further career advancement, after years of training and work. Moreover, at the same time that the Defense Department was dead-ending women's careers, it was attempting to secure authority to draft women as nurses, a "noncombat" job often performed in combat zones.

The signals are strong from the Pentagon that during periods of high unemployment, women are no longer needed to fill vacant volunteer slots. As in the past, women are the first to be turned away—denied the needed training, skills, and benefits for an economically secure future.

This unequal treatment is extended to spouses of military personnel, 95 percent of whom are women. A serious crisis occurs for many military wives during divorce because their husbands' pensions are not treated as marital property, divisible in the event of divorce. The military pension is the major asset accumulated during most military marriages; thus the divorced military wife is often left impoverished.

The transient life-style of the military family hardly gives the spouse an opportunity to build a lasting career or economic independence; indeed, the military actively discourages wives of officers, especially, from pursuing independent careers. It has a policy of rating "the whole man," which includes reviewing the performance of his wife in such "volunteer" activities as working in military-base thrift shops, attending the teas and coffees of the officers' wives' clubs, and entertaining junior officers and their wives under her husband's command. Any dereliction in these duties by an officer's wife may show up in *his* efficiency report and can affect his military career. Such practices either require the subordination of her career to his or totally discourage her from pursuing one, making her economically dependent on his salary during his active service, and on his pension in retirement as well. Thus the military's attitude toward the divisibility of pensions in case of divorce is all the more unjust.

For eight years, Congresswoman Patricia Schroeder (D-CO) had worked to enact legislation that would make military pensions marital property for divorce-settlement purposes. In June 1981, the Supreme Court ruled that current regulations *prohibited* military pensions to be divided in divorce settlements. Immediately after the decision, however, an organized effort, coordinated by military wives and aided by Capitol Hill's awareness of the gender gap, was successful in winning congressional enactment of legislation allowing state courts to consider military pensions as marital property during divorce. This solution—for each state to make its own case-by-case decisions on military pensions—is still a Band-Aid approach to solving the serious problems of ex–military wives.

Military spending, defense policies, and employment profiles repeatedly result in women losing out economically: Women in the military are discriminated against in jobs, promotions, and thereby in pay: military spouses are placed in economically precarious situations; and women in the civilian sector lose jobs with every increase in defense spending, because these increases necessitate sharp cuts in social-spending programs from which women and their families derive jobs and benefits.

These economic facts, together with women's alienation from the horrors of war, further explain the gender gap on defense spending and social spending. Indeed, war issues will be a major factor in future elections, and particularly when a national candidate is perceived as a "hawk." Women fear the potential of war and are highly suspicious of bellicose foreign-policy stands.

The New Right, which advocates a super defense program and extolls the value of "shows of force," is on a collision course with the deeply held convictions of the majority of women.

Women and Violence

Women's concerns about violence are not limited to the violence of war. For us, the issue of violence extends into the neighborhood— and, for a growing number of women, into the home.

When Gallup pollsters ask during door-to-door interviews, "Is there an area right around here, within a mile, where you would be afraid to walk alone at night?" three out of four women, but only one in four men, say yes.[19] And women's fears are well founded. One in every ten women in America is likely to be raped sometime during her life. And rape still remains one of the most underreported crimes today. Justice Department figures showed 178,000 rapes in 1981, but experts believe that for every rape reported, from 10 to 25 are not.[20]

Polls also show that more women favor social policies that would help eliminate violence. Women (by 12 points) say that they think there should be a law forbidding the private possession of handguns. Seventy-three percent of women, compared to half of the men surveyed, think our gun laws should be made stricter, with a majority of women wanting a ban on handguns.[21] But guns are not the most dangerous aspect of violence for women; violence for too many women begins in the home.

In a powerful 1983 cover story entitled "Private Violence," *Time* magazine explored the issues of child abuse, wife beating, and rape, calling these "a nightmarish realm only beginning to be forthrightly explored."[22]

Although reliable statistics do not exist, an estimated 1.8 million women are beaten each year by their husbands or lovers.[23] Several thousand of these females are beaten to death. Only one national study has ever been conducted on wife abuse, and according to this 1976 survey, these figures substantially underrepresent the extent of violence in American families by perhaps half.

Violence breeds violence. One in four people who grew up in homes with parents hitting children or each other uses some physical force on his/her spouse. One in ten husbands who grew up in violent homes severely assaults his wife.[24] These figures, too, are underrepresentative.

The lack of solutions and the fact that family violence impacts so many women today are reasons why these issues will take an increasingly prominent place in public policy debates as more females hold power. What *Time* calls a "private" form of violence is rapidly becoming a salient public issue.

When Ronald Reagan took office in January 1981, only about 400 shelters for battered women were in operation. An estimated 100 of these have since been shut down due to funding cuts and reversals in social-welfare programs.

There is no federal legislation on family violence, nor has there been a serious effort to enact any since 1980 when women suffered a crushing defeat from the New Right's blocking of a domestic-violence bill. But the gender gap could well change this. One struggle in particular shows how.

In 1978, Baltimore Congresswoman Barbara Mikulski first introduced into the U.S. House of Representatives the Domestic Violence Prevention and Services bill, which she describes as a "modest proposal to meet a tremendous problem." The bill, which has been introduced every year since, would provide about $65 million over a three-year period for domestic-violence shelters and other programs offering direct aid to battered women.[25]

Just prior to the 1980 elections, the domestic-violence bill passed both houses of Congress, with the slight differences between them ready to be resolved in the Conference Committee. And that's where the trouble began.

Opposition surfaced from the radical right wing of the Republican party. Senator Jesse Helms made statements about how the battered-women shelters would become "indoctrination centers." Other conservative senators also opposed the bill, advising that "the federal government should not interfere with family life."[26] Nevertheless, in October 1980, just before the presidential elections, the House passed the final version of the bill. The Senate, it was believed, would pass it after the elections, despite New Right opposition.

Then on Election Day 1980, when the Senate majority shifted to Republicans, thereby enhancing the power of the New Right, the bottom fell out on women's-rights legislation, eliminating the desperately needed battered-women shelters. The tide had turned. Ronald Reagan had been elected in what was perceived as a "landslide due to the country turning to the right." Postelection voting analyses, especially of women's votes, dispelled this myth, but it was too late for the domestic-violence bill.

In congressional sessions since 1980, the domestic-violence legislation has continued to be reintroduced. For 1984, there is new hope: Congressional sponsors, including Democrats George Miller (CA), Lindy Boggs (LA), and Mikulski, have developed a plan to attach the bill to a similar piece of legislation on abused children—legislation that has support from New Right senators.

Congressional observers cite three main reasons why this time the bill may pass.

First, the growing needs of battered women have received increased media attention, which in turn has further documented the problem.

Second, according to congressional aides, the gender gap will encourage both Republicans and Democrats to look for women's issues to support in 1984.

And third, Congress already seems more receptive to addressing the issue of women and violence. House Democrats have been bolder in their opposition to Reagan's budget cuts, and moderate Republican senators are bolting their party lines. Should the Democratic House pass Mikulski's legislation, it will be for the Republican Senate to decide, as with the ERA, where they really stand on one of the most basic of women's-rights issues.

As more attention is focused on the gender gap, Congress will be looking for some "safe" issues on which to build their "women's" record. Domestic violence could help fill the bill.

With so many issues of vital concern to women being neglected and women's opinions being ignored, the need for women to organize and dramatically increase their political clout has never been greater. Fortunately, women have been organizing for some time—we're not new to the game—and we are all the wiser because neither political party nor any major political institution has fulfilled its promises to women.

II

Women Weren't Born Democrat, Republican, or Yesterday

The Promise Broken
by Republicans

The attack on women's rights by the Reagan administration and the New Right has widened the gender gap, turning women away from the Republican party. Women's reaction has been vocal, strong, and unified. Determined not to lose two decades of progress in just four years, advocates of equality have fought each rollback of progress. Some attempted rollbacks have been halted in the courts and some in Congress, but most of the worst proposals have only been slowed down—just a few have been stopped. We have watched daily an administration slowly destroying programs that took years to put in place. Granted, some of these have never worked perfectly, but they did begin the process of advancement for women and minorities.

Many more people now understand that it is not only possible for women to lose hard-won ground, but that it can actually happen more quickly than we imagined.

None of this should come as a complete surprise. One of the most popular tomes of the Reagan Administration is George Gilder's *Wealth and Poverty*.[1] Reagan's budget director, David Stockman, hailed the book as "Promethean in its intellectual power and insight."

In this book, celebrated by supply-side economists and the New Right, Gilder asserts that there is no discrimination based on sex, and only a little, for men only, based on race. As to the problems faced by employed women, he claims that "equal pay for equal work is a principle that applies nowhere."[2] Gilder solemnly declares that upward mobility for minority men will be achieved (as he states it has for white men, who would otherwise also be unproductive, spendthrift members of society) when they have totally dependent wives and children as an incentive to inspire them to productivity.

From a presidential administration that takes such a book seriously, little should have been expected.

The Dismantling of Women's Rights

Under pressure from the women's-rights movement, considerable federal action was taken to reduce sex discrimination during the 1970s. Presidents Johnson, Nixon, Ford, and Carter issued executive orders or signed into law statutes providing for equal employment and education, and general programs advancing the rights of women. By 1975, funding began for centers providing services to rape victims, battered women, and displaced homemakers; and for projects supporting equality for girls and women in sports, the sciences, and throughout our educational system.

Words were stronger than actions: Most programs were underfunded, regulations were not vigorously enforced, and progress was slow. The Equal Rights Amendment, which would have added constitutional clout to the enforcement of these new laws, was stalled just a few states short of ratification. But at least there were programs working to eliminate discrimination. Progress, even at a snail's pace, was always in the direction of increased opportunity.

During the 1980 elections, both President Carter and candidate Ronald Reagan pledged themselves to the goals of equal rights and full opportunities for women. The Republican platform promised, "We will work vigorously to eradicate every remaining vestige of discrimination against women in state and federal laws." Part of Reagan's rhetoric during the 1980 campaign and continuing through his administration has been that he is for the "E" and the "R," but not the "A" of the Equal Rights Amendment—that is, he claims to support equal rights, but opposes a constitutional amendment as a way of achieving that goal.

Feminists were never fooled by this rhetoric. Nor were the activists who had spent any length of time in the drive for equal rights. We viewed Ronald Reagan as the titular leader of the New Right, which by 1980 had implanted its leaders and philosophies at the top of the Republican party and in the GOP platform, the U.S. Senate, and the White House. We knew from our state ERA campaigns that it was New Right advocates taking the lead in efforts opposing affirmative action in employment and education, while at the same time promoting the confinement of women, regardless of each woman's economic needs, in the exclusive role of wife and mother, subordinate to their husbands. Today, these same advocates are in policy positions in the Reagan administration.

Many were deceived by candidate Reagan's double-talk. But after several years of a Reagan administration and its New Right philosophies, fewer will be fooled in 1984.

The Reagan administration has from its very first days been attacking the most basic principles of equal rights for women. Throughout the federal government, officials of the Reagan administration, most of whom come from the ranks of the New Right, have systematically and thoroughly been moving to reverse the gains women have made over the last decade.

This war on women's rights has many aspects. First, there has been a continuous attack on the basic concepts of equality, such as affirmative action as a means of remedying past discrimination. Second, regulations enforcing equal employment and equal education have been narrowed in both coverage and applicability, resulting in many forms of discrimination going unchecked. Third, rather than working to eliminate discrimination system-wide and thus helping the largest number of women, the Republican administration has adopted a case-by-case, individual-by-individual approach. Fourth, funding of enforcement programs has been cut severely or eliminated altogether. And five, time and again those appointed by Reagan to take the responsibility for eliminating discrimination are the very same people who oppose the concepts of equal rights and full equality.

The focusing of attention on the gender gap has caused the administration and conservative Republican leaders to be slightly more sensitive about their public statements on women. Behind closed doors, however, they continue to pursue policies resulting in massive losses for women in their jobs, educational opportunities, and overall economic security.

Briefly, here's how these policies work.

Attacking the Basic Concepts of Equality

Since the passage of civil-rights laws in the mid-1960s, conservatives and business interests have attempted to discredit the intent and effect of affirmative action. They have clearly used inflammatory language to confuse the American public and create hostility for such programs. By claiming affirmative action is really "reverse discrimination" against white males, and by asserting that "mandatory quotas" will obligate employers to hire unqualified female or black applicants, opponents of equality try to capitalize on people's fears.[3]

The fact is that both "reverse discrimination" and "mandatory quotas" are phony issues. The laws and regulations concerning affirmative action never required "mandatory quotas," no civil-rights group ever pressed for their imposition, and none has ever been required by enforcement agencies. The phrase *reverse discrimination* was the invention of a propagandist skilled in the techniques of the "divide and conquer" strategy.

Why is affirmative action so maligned? I believe it is because discrimination is profitable.

The term *affirmative action* was first used by President Johnson to describe the importance of taking steps to cure past injustices. Based on the assumption that an employer ultimately supports an integrated work force, affirmative-action plans outline an orderly and reasonable method of achieving this goal. Affirmative-action programs include steps an employer or educational institution may take to remedy past discrimination on the basis of sex, race, national origin, or physical disability. Suggested measures are posting job openings and recruiting in a manner that will actually reach out to minorities and women, as well as to white males. The essence of affirmative action is that employers take deliberate steps to consider qualified people who have traditionally been excluded from consideration for certain job categories in the work force.

To be effective, an affirmative-action plan must contain goals and timetables so the program can be evaluated and improved. Goals and timetables were added to affirmative-action plans after the federal government had spent several years trying to enforce antidiscrimination laws with little or no success. By no curious coincidence, without goals and timetables, white male employers continued to claim that the only "truly qualified" people they could find, especially for higher-paying jobs, were their own mirror images: white males. Countless cases have proved, time and time again, that this bias was the principal basis on which employers rejected otherwise totally qualified female and minority applicants. Ideally, affirmative action is a temporary plan, to be used until reasonable integration of a company's work force has been achieved.

These programs have proved to be an effective means of achieving equality. Study after study shows that affirmative-action plans, the types criticized by President Reagan and the New Right, have been highly effective in promoting the employment of women, blacks, and Hispanics. These programs also have high levels of support among Americans in general and women in particular. Seventy percent of people favor federal laws requiring affirmative-action employment plans for women and minorities, provided there are no rigid quotas.[4]

The most efficient affirmative-action plans are those in which the decision to integrate a company's work force is made at the highest policymaking levels. Such orders are rarely given. I can still remember a 1972 conversation with a high-ranking officer of a major bank in Pittsburgh. He admitted to several of us that his bank discriminated on the basis of sex: Two-thirds of the bank's employees were women, who were paid 60 percent of what the men were paid. After World War II, he explained, bank tellers were mostly men; then the decision was made to make these jobs lower-paying ones with no upward mobility. Women were gradually hired to fill the bank-teller positions. "After all, how many officers can you have in a bank?" he asked. "But," he added, "if the chairman of the board gave an order to end discrimination in hiring and pay, it could be done immediately, plan or no plan."

Ronald Reagan and members of his administration ignore both the public's support of affirmative action and its positive results. Conservative policymakers seem never to talk of affirmative action without coupling it with the false stigma of mandatory quotas or reverse discrimination.

Reagan's retreat from affirmative action not only is stopping progress for women, but is reversing it. Both employed women and those someday planning to take paid jobs have a vested interest in the success of affirmative action and future enforcement efforts. They also are the victims of the Reagan administration's actions in these areas, actions contributing to the overall perception that this administration is unfair to women.

Narrowing the Regulations

A second technique the New Right uses to blunt the drive for women's equality is the redefining and narrowing of antidiscrimination laws, regulations, and programs already in existence—particularly the equal-education programs and the employment rules for federal contractors.

Title IX of the Education Amendments of 1972 prohibits sex discrimination in federally funded educational programs. All previous administrations have supported equal-education policies that define Title IX as covering an *entire* institution—e.g., a college or university receiving funds, not just the specific program. These policies were first developed during the Nixon administration when Caspar Weinberger (now Reagan's secretary of defense) served as secretary of health, education, and welfare.

The Reagan administration, however, has reversed these long-standing policies for equal education. During the summer of 1983, at the same time Reagan was defending his record on women's rights in speeches, his Department of Justice was preparing a frontal attack on Title IX, claiming it prohibited sex discrimination in only those programs *directly* funded by the federal government. In the case of *Grove City College* v. *Bell,* the administration for the first time argued that *only* the financial-aid department of Grove City College (not the entire college)—because it received the money for student loans from the federal government—must comply with Title IX.[5]

This argument raised a storm of protest among both Republicans and Democrats in Congress. Claudine Schneider (R-RI), along with 50 other members of Congress, including Senator Robert Dole (R-KS), submitted an *amicus* brief challenging the administration's position and asserting that the legislative history of Title IX shows that an *entire* institution is prohibited from discriminating when it receives federal funds, and that there is "overwhelming evidence" that Congress intended a broad reading and "comprehensive application" of the law.[6]

The Reagan administration's position, if accepted by the Supreme Court, not only will gut Title IX but could be extended to some 51 other laws with similar wording. In this one radical move, Reagan has launched a frontal assault on measures that prohibit discrimination against women, minorities, and the handicapped.

In the area of equal-employment enforcement, rollbacks are too numerous to detail. The Reagan administration has taken numerous steps to reverse the decade-long progress toward increasing the number of women working for government contractors.

Under the guise of relieving business of excessive regulation and easing their paper work, the Reagan administration is pushing through new regulations for the Office of Federal Contract Compliance Programs (OFCCP) in the U.S. Department of Labor. These changes mean that 70 percent of the companies doing business as federal contractors are exempted from developing affirmative-action plans. In addition, third-party complaints of discrimination—for example, those filed by NOW or civil-rights groups—have been made extremely difficult; and in cases in which discrimination exists, awards of back pay will be extremely limited, if not denied. In short, businesses that are awarded federal contracts sometimes amounting to hundreds of millions of dollars will not need to make much of an effort to employ women or minorities to meet minimum government standards.

Eliminating Discrimination, Individual by Individual

Upon taking office in 1981, top officials in the Reagan Justice Department made clear their intentions of reversing progress for women by announcing that the government would no longer initiate class-action cases challenging discrimination. They claimed the administration would proceed on an individual-by-individual basis to eliminate job bias.

By definition, discrimination is a class problem affecting large numbers of female workers. To prove discrimination in a court of law, the use of statistics is essential. Curing discrimination by challenging job bias individual by individual will not only take forever, it will be nearly impossible to do through court cases.

The first thing a company or educational institution does in defending itself against a discrimination case is to try to discredit the individual who filed the suit. If that party can't be exposed as incompetent, or insubordinate, or a drunkard, then the usual tactic is to insinuate that she has a "personality problem."

It doesn't take a Perry Mason to raise enough doubts about an individual (or an individual's work) to lead even her closest friends to question whether it was a case of discrimination or just her personality.

However, when statistical evidence is introduced, it becomes not just a case of one vulnerable individual but a question of whether a *system* of discrimination exists against any given *group* of individuals. Evidence of such a pattern of practices is usually essential unless the individual can show a "smoking gun"—for example, a memo that actually states the employee was denied a promotion because of being female.

A more serious concern, however, is the Justice Department's change in policies on class-action cases, which makes such cases more difficult to litigate. Class-action lawsuits are very expensive for individuals or small groups of women to take to the courts.

Cases were previously fought by the federal government on behalf of women who as a group suffered job discrimination at AT&T, General Electric, and other large companies. These class-action suits helped thousands of women. Now, however, the burden of bringing such suits falls upon those who are already victims of discrimination, or upon women's rights groups with budgets stretched thin by other Reagan administration rollbacks.

Cutting Enforcement Funding

As we have seen, women's progress has been reversed by the government's extensive policy changes, the narrowing of regulations, and the filing of fewer and less substantive court cases on discrimination. Underlying all these setbacks have been corresponding budget cuts that undermine the government's ability to enforce existing laws and to challenge sex and race biases. Enforcement programs in the departments of Labor and Education have suffered radical budget reductions, as has the Equal Employment Opportunity Commission. Thus, while the administration is trying to dilute the equal-rights laws by court cases that will restrict their scope (as in the Grove City Title IX suit), it is also making equal-opportunity enforcement nearly impossible.

Appointing Opponents to Administer Equal Rights

A consistent pattern has emerged in Reagan's appointments to civil-rights enforcement agencies: The appointees usually are opposed to the basic concepts of equal rights, including affirmative action and aggressive enforcement of antidiscrimination laws. In fact, many of these policymakers, prior to their appointments, built their track records in New Right organizations by fighting women's rights.

One example is the solicitor general of the U.S. Department of Justice, Rex E. Lee. He is the second-in-command and the lawyer who takes all cases to the Supreme Court on behalf of the government. Prior to his appointment, Lee authored a book, *A Lawyer Looks at the Equal Rights Amendment,*[7] in which he claimed the ERA should be defeated: "the risks entailed in the proposed 27th Amendment [ERA] are not worth running because the need for massive change is not great. . . ." As solicitor general, Lee has argued for further restrictions on affirmative action, abortion, and reproductive rights, and he was one of the chief architects in the Grove City case. Similar New Right appointments have been made throughout the departments of Justice, Education, and Labor, the Office of Management and Budget, the Equal Employment Opportunity Commission, and the U.S. Commission on Civil Rights.

Yet another administration technique for stifling women's progress is to leave critical agency positions vacant. In the case of the Equal Employment Opportunity Commission, the administration did not bother to appoint a chairperson or enough commissioners to make a quorum for nearly a year.

Perceptions and Realities

Not only does Ronald Reagan have a gender-gap problem, but women's negative ratings are extending to the Republican party in general.

The warning signs have been in the air since the 1980 elections. Senator Bob Packwood, a Republican from the state of Oregon, was the first to publicly challenge his party to face the new realities posed by a women's voting bloc. "The Republican party has just about written off those women who work for wages in the marketplace," he told Republican leaders. "We are losing them in droves. You cannot write them off and the blacks off and the Hispanics off and the Jews off and assume you are going to build a party on white Anglo-Saxon males over forty."[8]

Reagan's response to women's criticism has often been one of puzzlement. "Benign bewilderment in response to the women's revolution is a license for bigotry at every level and in every quarter of the land, and that is the lesson of the last three years of the Reagan Administration," Republican Patricia Bailey told the National Women's Political Caucus.[9]

Is it any wonder that the chair of the National Women's Political Caucus, Kathy Wilson, a Republican, in the summer of 1983 said, "Mr. President, one term is enough. For the sake of American women —Republicans, Democrats, and Independents—please step down. Do not seek the Republican nomination. Four years is enough. As a matter of fact, it's entirely too much."

In many ways President Reagan has become a symbol to women of the insensitivities of New Right policies. And as long as the Republicans continue to sanction radical right-wing spokesmen with top political positions, the GOP will alienate women. With massive defections by women, the Republicans run the risk of forever being relegated to minority-party status.

The stakes for women—and for the Republicans—are indeed high in the 1984 elections.

The Party Dilemma:
What Real Choice for Women?

The feminist movement has been blessed with quick wits and marvelous slogans—and none better than Women Weren't Born Democrat, Republican, or Yesterday. In one phrase, it says it all: Women cannot be taken for granted by either political party and they cannot be fooled by them.

In June 1982, the women's movement was ending the ERA Countdown Campaign, knowing that Republicans had deserted the ERA. Some 83 percent of Republican legislators in key unratified states had voted against the amendment. Republicans in the White House, Congress, and the state legislatures were the leaders of the ERA opposition.

Yet neither had Democrats done all they should have done. Many women had spent ten years begging Democrats to do more and to place the ERA higher on their agenda—all to little avail. The ERA was defeated in Democrat-controlled Oklahoma, Florida, and North Carolina. True, all Republican senators in North Carolina and Oklahoma had voted "no" on the ERA, and 10 out of 12 in Florida had voted "no," but only about 55 percent of the Democrats in these states had voted "yes." Several key leaders of the opposition to the ERA in these states were Democrats, notably Senator Dempsey Barron, dean of the Florida Senate; and Lieutenant Governor Jimmy Green of North Carolina, president of the North Carolina Senate. In other words, Democratic support was neither solid nor strong enough for victory even in Democratic states.

The same picture holds true for other women's issues. Leading opponents of women's right of access to abortion are Democrats as well as Republicans. The 1983 attempt to pass a constitutional amendment permitting Congress and/or the states to ban abortion was cosponsored by Senator Orrin Hatch (R-UT) *and* Thomas Eagleton (D-MO). This measure was defeated 50–49 (a two-thirds majority was needed for passage), with 34 Republicans and 15 Democrats supporting it and 19 Republicans and 31 Democrats opposing it.[1] The floor leader for the "pro-choice" side—to preserve access to legal and safe abortions—was Republican Senator Robert Packwood of Oregon.

A close look at America's two parties, of course, frequently reveals *four* parties: conservative Democrats (boll weevils), who are aligned with New Right Republicans on women's economic issues, including ERA, versus moderate to liberal Democrats, who are closely aligned with liberal Republicans (gypsy moths). But frequently women's issues cannot be analyzed even along these conservative-moderate-liberal lines, which transcend party identification. For example, Senator Eagleton, a Democrat, and Senator Mark Hatfield, an Oregon Republican, are both moderates who favor outlawing abortions.

Women have a right to be dissatisfied with the performance of both political parties. Right-wing Republicans are obviously the opposition, but Democrats have not been strong enough champions. Too often we recognized that, given the radical-right orientation of the Republican party in recent years, Democratic leaders and analysts took us for granted, believing our only choice was the Democrats.

But what good was a choice that also led to defeat? To be damned with faint praise was still to be damned. It is no comfort for those of us determined to win equality for women.

Feminists certainly do not want to maintain the status quo (conservative) or return to the days of yesteryear (reactionary). Since feminists advocate change, the frequent assumption is that they must be leftists. But feminists have not been comfortable with the Left, which is dominated by males who also ignore women's concerns and downgrade women's issues and status.

Political analyses of the American women's movement have for the most part ignored this inherent tension and simply labeled the movement "leftist," an assumption that leads many to see feminists primarily as liberal Democrats. Republicans thus feel they need not worry about these women because they are Democrats anyway, and Democrats feel they need not worry about these women because they are already Democrats and can be taken for granted. The leaders of both parties assume there is really nowhere else these women can go politically.

The assumptions are false. Feminist ideas cross old lines—for one simple reason: The Left, the Right, and the middle in politics have all been dominated by men, who all too frequently are content to ignore women.

Women simply do not view many of their political issues along old

"Left-Right" lines. In fact, many women's issues have only belatedly been viewed as political. Actually, feminists, like most women, are not strongly party-identified, and party lines seem largely irrelevant to them. Many women are suspicious of both political parties and view themselves as "independents."

They see neither party as a vehicle for women's rights nor representative of their views. Leaders of the feminist movement, as well as leaders of more traditional women's organizations, tend to be women who have not been active in political organizations.

Politicizing Women's-Rights Issues

In the late 1960s and early 1970s, the key women's-rights issues were viewed as bipartisan or even nonpartisan. Both Democratic and Republican officeholders, for example, supported the ERA in 1972, when it was passed by Congress, as did every president—Republican and Democrat—until Ronald Reagan. Both parties seemed supportive of family planning and individual choice in reproductive matters. Both seemed to be in favor of affirmative action to end discrimination in employment and education. Throughout the 1970s, there seemed to be little difference between the parties on women's issues.

Women leaders worked to keep women's issues bipartisan. We stressed that both Republicans and Democrats supported our issues and that pro-ERA and pro-choice groups included prominent Republicans and prominent Democrats.

Frequently, politicians have stated that women's issues are not political issues; rather they have said they are moral issues. They claim these were personal issues, matters of religion and moral conviction. Often women's-rights activists were advised that the normal party "whip" system could not be employed on one or another women's issue because it involved the deep religious commitment of a legislator. On women's issues—unlike most others—how a legislator or his wife viewed a matter personally was enough; the party could demand no loyalty, and constituents simply had to understand.

Both the women's movement and the New Right have been changing all this. The feminist movement was quick to realize that most of its key issues were being decided in the political arena and, hence, regardless of how some sought to explain away their political aspects, these issues were inherently political in nature—public policy was determining the rights of women. The feminists believed that women's issues were interpreted as personal only to mask their political nature.

The feminist movement sought to "politicize" its issues in the minds of women. What happened to you during your divorce, we argued, was shaped by public policy determined in state legislatures and interpreted by the courts. It was not a personal matter but a matter of public policy that your contributions as a homemaker were not considered as important as your husband's paycheck. We needed political power to make the laws more equitable for us.

At approximately the same time, the New Right was also politicizing and polarizing women's issues. With the New Right's domination of the Republican party in the 1980s, the bipartisanship of women's issues of the 1970s has all but disappeared. In fact, the New Right used opposition to women's-rights issues as an organizing device. Openly taking on the fight against the ERA, abortion, and affirmative action for women and minorities in employment and education, while fighting to preserve white male supremacy, the New Right organized those fearful of change.

The New Right coined the phrase *reverse discrimination* to condemn as an attack on white males any program that helped women and minorities gain equity in educational and job opportunities. Feminists asserted in turn that white males had been the privileged beneficiaries of their own affirmative-action program from one generation to the next for centuries.

New Right advocates played upon modern-day fears about the "crisis of the family" by blaming feminists for divorce and the breakup of the family. (Actually, the rise of modern feminism postdates the rise of the divorce rate.) The New Right represented itself as the anointed custodian not only of superpatriotism and the flag, but of the American family as well. All equitable changes sought for women became an attack on the family. In the New Right's view, nothing could be allowed to interfere with a man's right to dominate his family. Not only legislation to protect battered wives but child-abuse legislation designed to protect abused children was attacked as "antifamily."

One of the most prominent New Right leaders, Howard Phillips, chairman of the Conservative Caucus, has gone so far in his extreme notion of "the family" that he accused the government of promoting antifamily policies since the nineteenth century. "It has been a conscious policy of government to liberate the wife from the leadership of the husband and thus break up the family as a unit of government." As one example, he cited legislation in the 1800s giving married women property rights. He also pointed to the fact that women have been liberated from the political leadership of their husbands. "You know, it used to be that in recognition of the family as a basic unit of society, we had one family, one vote. And we have seen the trend instead toward one person, one vote."[2]

Phillips viewed the married woman's property act as an encroachment on men's right to control all money in the family (including money the wife might have earned or inherited, which is what this nineteenth-century legislation addressed); and he saw woman suffrage—permitting women to vote—as an encroachment upon men's right to control the political arena. New Right men seem extraordinarily determined to exercise power, if not in public life, then certainly in private.

But the New Right's vitriolic attack on women's issues and the women's movement does not mean the Democrats have suddenly seen the light. If the New Right took up the fight against women's rights, no male group took up the challenge to defend women's rights. We feminists were largely on our own defending women's rights, watching many Democrats reap a windfall they did not harvest. The New Right did make one major contribution: It hastened the politicalization of women's issues. No longer did anyone argue with feminists whether women's issues, like abortion and divorce, were political issues, the rules of which were being shaped in the political arena—in the legislatures and the courts. The male New Right did for women's issues what the women's movement perhaps could not have done alone: It helped place women's-rights issues at the center stage of American politics.

Ironically, the lack of adequate Democratic male response to the New Right attack against women's rights has also provided an invaluable service to women. After repeatedly turning in vain to the male elected Democrats to save the ERA or abortion rights, women activists began increasingly to turn to themselves. Never has the women's movement been so united or determined to increase the number of women in office.

The Political Reality: Too Little Representation of Women

Women activists of all kinds and all political persuasions have one common complaint: We are ignored and our issues are trivialized by male political leaders. Women's interests in such issues as family planning, divorce, affirmative action in jobs and education, child care, wife battering, and child support have not been adequately represented in the decision-making of political parties, legislatures, city

halls, courts, Congress, or the White House, all of which are dominated by men and their interests.

I'll never forget sitting in family court in the early 1970s as a
participant in a project of the Domestic Relations Committee of
Pittsburgh NOW. It was Christmastime, and the male judge was
routinely saying to men who were defaulting in child-support payments that because it was the Christmas season, he would forgive
them for being in arrears.

"What about the women and children?" I wanted to cry out.

I will never forget, also, one patronizing, older male judge who
"comforted" a desperate woman by saying, "After all, my dear, you
can remarry."

We women who watched this scene were appalled: "Does he expect
her to marry just anyone? When? This minute as a convenience for
her ex-husband and the judge?"

That kind of nightmare continues to this day. After divorce,
women's income plummets (by 73 percent), but men's income goes up
(by 42 percent).[3] Recently, the U.S. Census Bureau released a 1982
survey revealing that less than half (47 percent) of the women with
children under 21 who are awarded child support ever receive full
payments. Only about one-third (35 percent) of the fathers make full
or partial payment of child support.

Too often the decisions rendered by male judges are based on
sympathy with the old (male) adage, "Why should he contribute to
a dead horse?" How often have you heard women say of men, "They
don't get the point, and they don't want to. They don't understand.
Why should they? They like the system the way it is."

I was constantly reminded of female underrepresentation in the
state legislatures when I was campaigning for the ERA. In the spring
of 1982 in Tallahassee, Florida, a bill had been brought to the floor
of the Florida Senate that would require a husband to be notified if
his wife was going to have an abortion.

Senator Pat Frank (D-Tampa) was tired of hearing this Democrati-
cally controlled, essentially all-male Senate debate the rights of
women, so she proposed an amendment to the Bill. The amendment
required a man who impregnated a woman other than his wife to
notify his wife if the other woman was going to have an abortion.
"What's good for the goose is good for the gander," reasoned Senator
Frank.

Interestingly, her amendment, which of course failed overwhelmingly in a *voice* vote, lost by only two votes when she demanded a
roll-call vote. Many senators who had voted by voice left the floor

("hit the doors") when they knew their vote against the amendment was going to be recorded. Even more interesting, the original bill was also withdrawn, because the president of the Senate thought the Senate was being made to look foolish.

I first heard of this legislative drama as I was walking up to the Capitol that day. A young woman ran over to me yelling, "You've missed it! It was so wonderful—we were all laughing at them!"

As the word had spread through the Capitol, the galleries had filled rapidly with women, who enjoyed seeing the tables turned for once on the male senators.

Senator Frank said afterward that instead of fighting constantly for women's rights, she would try to amend bills that were unfair to women so they would have an equally unfair impact on men. She hoped that maybe, at last, her male colleagues would begin to understand.

Why do female legislators have to go to such extremes to make male legislators understand? Why do women legislators frequently feel they have "to carry the water" for women's issues? Why do they so often feel isolated—not a part of "the men's club" of the legislature?

I believe it's for the same reason that most women do not feel a deep party loyalty: They are ignored by male-dominated structures. The woman legislator is still treated as an anomaly—as a *woman* legislator, not just a legislator. She is *not* treated as one of the "good ole boys," and typically is not in a position of power.

Only 12 percent of state legislators and less than 5 percent of members of Congress are female. Or, to put it in the reverse, men comprise 94 percent of all state senators, 86 percent of all state representatives, 98 percent of U.S. senators, and 95 percent of U.S. representatives. But the percentages of women, small as they are, actually inflate women's influence in these legislatures. If the positions of power—e.g., Speaker of the House, president of the Senate, chairs of key committees—were analyzed, the percentage of women would shrink to an infinitesimal number.

The atmosphere of American legislatures is extremely male-biased and unrepresentative of women. When serious issues, such as wife beating, are being discussed, some immature legislators make derisive, supposedly funny comments, and too many others join in the laughter.

Throughout the ERA campaign, it was open season for sexual slurs and jokes among those legislators unable to shed their adolescent behavior. The jokes had a bitter sort of irony in the context of statehouses rife with gossip about the extramarital affairs of many of the legislators. Those who most ardently preached the traditional values and the sanctity of the family were also among those who were all too human. And there were also legislators who were rumored to engage in wife beating or child abuse; how were feminists to convince *them* of the importance of women's issues?

During the 1982 campaign, one governor from a key state told me a particular senator was the linchpin that would swing the vote our way. We had to get his vote. He suggested we work that senator's district.

I said, "Surely, governor, you can't be serious—he's been married four times, he's widely known for beating his current wife."

The governor's voice dropped. He said, "I know. He's an animal."

I said, "Forget it."

The atmosphere was and remains all wrong for women to be taken seriously. Women in this domain are mostly underpaid office workers, or those of us who come here to be cheerleaders. The players are men —voting on matters that affect the lives of all of us. The women legislators, present in such limited numbers on "male turf," are themselves frequently victims of sex discrimination.

Of course there are fine, decent male legislators, who are champions of women's rights. Every time I say how important it is to have more women elected, I remember how important it is also to have men like Congressman Don Edwards (D-CA), who has been chief sponsor of the ERA in the U.S. House for more than a decade. Yet we need more women officeholders to create an atmosphere in which women and their issues are treated seriously and fairly.

Do Women Officeholders Care More About Women's Issues?

Early in my work on women's issues, I believed differences in attitudes on women's issues would be based on the political ideologies of legislators, not on their gender. But like most political analysts, I was fooled. Female legislators tend to care more about women's issues than do male legislators, regardless of their political philosophy. For example, while less than half (46 percent) of the male legislators in key un-ratified states favored the ERA, 75 percent of the female legislators were for it.[4]

In 1978, the Center for the American Woman and Politics (CAWP) conducted a national survey of women and men in public office.[5] Their findings confirm my experience and that of countless other legislators and political activists that I have talked with on this subject: Women officeholders favor women's issues more than their male counterparts do. The Center's findings, which are derived from 16 states at the state legislative and county levels and 8 states at the mayoral and council levels, reveal even stronger support for the ERA among female legislators than we observed in the unratified states. In these states, 96 percent of the women state senators and 82 percent of the women state representatives favored the ERA. When the Center held political philosophy constant, in every instance women favored women's issues more than their male counterparts did.

Women in office both increase the level of support for women's issues and change the atmosphere. Women officeholders not only vote more for women's issues but often lead the fight for them. They are usually the initiators of the legislation, or among its prime sponsors. Most important, they do the vote-counting for these issues and are willing to "trade" votes for them. Women's-rights bills are important to these women, so they work closely with women's and civic groups for their passage. They know their female constituents expect them to fight for them—they know they are among those few who are willing "to carry the water" for women—and they take on the challenge again and again as their special duty. What's more, their male colleagues know the legislation is important to them.

Even when women legislators do not initiate women's legislation, their very presence suggests it. No sooner had state representative Bonnie Brown and state senator Sandra Lucht been elected to the West Virginia state legislature, in 1982, than a bill was enacted requiring that nonsexist language be used in legislation. Shortly thereafter, a bill providing for a more equitable property division for women in divorce was introduced. Although both women were active feminists and, in fact, past state coordinators of NOW, they did not initiate either bill. There is no question in their minds, however, that their victories in winning elected positions, and their very presence, stimulated their male colleagues to introduce these and other changes for women.

I have found that too many male politicians do not understand why an issue is important to women. Frequently, they equate all women with their wives, mothers, or daughters. Women officeholders, on the other hand, not only understand but will frequently explain to others why it is important. The study conducted by the Center for the American Woman and Politics revealed that 47 percent of the women officeholders, as compared to only 8 percent of the men, had been employed in traditionally "female" occupations, such as teaching, nursing, secretarial and social work.[6] No study is necessary to conclude that even fewer men had ever had the experience of being homemakers.

During these years of working for women's rights, I was reminded frequently of the American Revolutionary slogan No Taxation Without Representation. Right now, women are not really represented in these legislative bodies; they are largely outsiders *begging* male insiders for their rights. Can you imagine lobbying an almost all-male legislative body, composed of many contemplating divorce, on a bill to provide more equitable divorce laws for women? Or, better yet, lobbying an almost all-male Congress to provide more-equitable pension programs for the spouses of federal workers, such as prorating pension rights for the divorced spouse? Congresswoman Patricia Schroeder has been trying to establish such pension rights for the past decade.

The few women inside need help. Soon. There must be no more begging. More women must run for office, and all of us must vote smarter—first, to increase the number of women in office and thus ensure serious consideration of women's issues and, second, to increase the numbers of both men and women officeholders committed to women's issues and equality. Candidates and officeholders do differ on issues—though many often seek to blur the differences—and the stakes are high for American women.

Women Can Be the Winning Edge

Knowing what is at stake—what women can win or lose—in the political arena is just one-half, albeit a crucial half, of the story concerning the need for women to organize politically. The other, perhaps more important half is knowing how you and other women and men who care can be effective. What can you do to safeguard and extend your rights personally—and women's rights generally?

Many people think you need a great deal of money, time, and status to be effective in the political arena. That may be true—especially if you do it alone. But there is no reason for you to do it alone.

Political parties are just one of the avenues of input in the American political system. Another avenue, which is increasing in importance today as the influence of the political parties wanes, is the "interest group," or "pressure group." Interest-group politics is as old as the American political system itself. There are interest groups representing business; labor; women; the environment; farmers; professional trade associations; churches; peace; civil rights; gay men and lesbians; ethnic groups; veterans; etc.

The political parties work to create an overall agenda, a consensus of priorities, for a variety of different interests—e.g., labor, farm groups, blacks, business, as well as the general public. Each political party tries to present both the whole and the parts according to that party's beliefs about how government should be run.

Interest groups each represent a particular segment of interests and people in the community as a whole. In the case of women's rights and interests, it is a very large segment, indeed.

Today many warn that interest-group politics is dangerous, polarizing, and neglectful of the common interest. The fact remains, however, that they are also empowering for the average person who has a particular concern in the political process. Interest groups represent real people and real concerns that may not be adequately represented otherwise. And for those who have been traditionally neglected or underrepresented by both elected officials and the political parties, interest groups provide an avenue of access to power and decision-making.

Women's groups, or groups representing women's interests, including female-only and female/male memberships, are not new. Many of them were formed in the first wave of the feminist movement to gain women's suffrage. Others were formed as auxiliaries to men's groups that excluded women. Still others were formed around occupations that are predominantly "female." Many of the women-only membership groups are primarily social, but a large faction engage in community activities.[7] Some are purely issue or public affairs oriented. Of course, the latest addition to the women's organizations are the women's-rights or feminist groups formed in the post–1960s and 1970s.

Women's groups are not newcomers to the governmental lobbying process. As early as 1929, a study of group representation before Congress reported women's groups were second in number only to trade associations.[8] And with the second wave of feminism, the number of women's groups has increased. Of course, so have the numbers of many other groups. Whatever the head count of groups, there is no question that women's groups of today, especially with the power of the gender gap, are more influential than they were some ten to twenty years ago.

There is such a wide variety of groups that an individual can pick and choose. Most women's interest groups have low annual membership fees that entitle the member to a group periodical publication. The various literatures can keep you up-to-date on women's issues.

Many people don't want to join groups, because they don't have the time to be active. But your membership fee pays for others to work

full-time at the problem and provides you with constant representation. Most groups permit their members to give as much or as little
time as each member can afford.

Another reason some people shy away from groups is that, while
they like some aspects of a particular group's program, they don't like
other aspects. No group will be perfect, but ask yourself whether those
you are interested in advance the status of women and whether they
deserve your support. If the answer is yes, join.

If no, start a group yourself. Starting a group is easier than it
appears. The next chapter will provide tips on how to start political-
action committees. One of the best ways of learning how to start and
run a group is by joining one you like and learning from the inside
how such a group is run. Before starting anything new, one must
know the ropes—and the best way to know organizations is to join
an existing organization.

Some large and well-funded organizations have amazing track records. Although an overwhelming majority of the population is for
handgun control, the lobby of the National Rifle Association, representing over 1 million members, has managed to defeat the majority
time and time again. No women's-rights organization is as big as the
National Rifle Association—yet surely women deserve a larger voice
than guns in our Congress. Look at the resource section of this book.
Pick an organization or several and send for their literature. It could
make a difference for you and women everywhere.

Women can be the winning edge by organizing together in pressure
groups. But they can also be the winning edge by becoming directly
involved in politics. One of the best ways is to pick candidates and
take an active part in their campaigns. Most political activists become
involved in just this way. Or, choose a political party and become
involved. The latter route is tougher for women because of male
domination of the parties, but, given the decline of party influence in
American politics, it is not necessary to come up through the party.
Few politicians at the top depend on the party for their start or their
campaigns anymore. Aim high; don't get dead-ended in traditional
"women's work." Pinpoint the jobs that have upward mobility, and
go for them.

Better yet, if you've already been involved in groups, campaigns, or
community work, think about running for political office yourself. If
you know your constituency is underrepresented and you could represent it, run. Don't think of the ideal qualifications for the job; think
of who has been serving in the office: Can you do a better job, or as
good a job, or an adequate job, and bring to the work the perspective

of women? If you can, you are badly needed in elected office.

Finally, every woman can be part of the gender gap by voting for the candidate who is closest to her viewpoints. There are many excuses not to vote: "There are no *real* choices," "My one vote doesn't count," and so on. But there *are* choices in many races, even when no candidate is exactly what you want. Voting for the lesser of two evils is still voting for the better of two candidates. And many elections are very close. If women are ever to be taken seriously politically, they must vote blatant anti–women's-rights candidates out of office or out of the running.

So often it is said women cannot play "hardball" politics. (Once again we are told what we cannot do.) Not only can we, I believe we are currently the fastest-growing and already largest potential interest group in the nation. I know many of us are fed up with being ignored.[9] I wrote the next section on women organizing because I believe women are more ready than ever before to lead. We have a vision of what the world should be like, and we are willing to fight for it.

III

Getting Organized

PAC Women: Fund-Raising
for Campaign Dollars

The essential ingredient of any successful campaign is money—enough, that is, for an adequate campaign treasury. While a candidate's personality, attractiveness, name recognition, and all other ingredients of a sound campaign strategy are important, without money a campaign cannot get to first base. Of course, candidates occasionally win even though they are outspent by their opponents. But generally the candidate who spends the most wins the race. Even those candidates who are outspent and win usually have spent an average amount for the offices they are seeking.

Just how much is "enough" varies from office to office and from one locale to another. To campaign for United States senator, a candidate will usually need more than $1 million and often as much as several million dollars. Local campaigns can sometimes be waged for a few hundred or a few thousand dollars, but even local or state races can be extremely expensive. State legislative races require from a few thousand dollars to $500,000, but the positions, once won, pay only modestly. The cost of running varies widely, but in most cases you cannot play the game of politics seriously without having money or being able to raise it.

If you're running for office yourself or supporting a candidate and don't have money, here is how to raise it.

Political Action Committees (PACs): How They Work

Political action committees can be a major source of funds. In dealing with them, it is important to know why they exist and how they work.

Until the past decade or so, women's organizations had stayed out of electoral politics. They advocated issues, educated the public, and lobbied their legislators, but they did not get involved in partisan politics or elections. Many women's groups feared that involvement in partisan politics might cost them their tax-exempt, nonprofit status.

Then two important developments occurred simultaneously in the 1970s. First, women's organizations learned a major lesson from their intense lobbying for women's issues, especially for the Equal Rights Amendment: They learned that effective lobbying begins with effective electoral activity; and that in elections, campaign money is essential. Second, during the 1970s, election laws were changed, permitting nonprofit organizations to participate in elections by establishing separate funds, commonly called "political action committees."

The new election laws, adopted at the federal level and by many states, allowed organizations to sponsor political action committees to raise funds for supporting electoral activity or for contributing to political candidates. The sponsoring organizations (just like corporations and unions) cannot themselves participate directly in any financial way in political campaigns, but they can set up separate funds—political action committees—that can. An organization cannot use its dues money or other organization funds to make a political contribution. This is against the law. But the organization can use its general funds to pay the administrative expenses of its PAC, such as salaries, rent, phones, and fund-raising costs; and the PAC in turn can contribute to candidates' campaigns and conduct other electoral activity with the proceeds from its fund-raising. PACs do not have to be affiliated with (or sponsored by) an organization; but for an organization to contribute directly to campaigns or electoral activity beyond its membership, it must have a PAC.

How to Organize a PAC

The legal steps for forming a political action committee are relatively simple. To start a PAC, an organization or collection of individuals generally must (1) fill out a statement of organization, (2) list the name of a chairperson and treasurer, and (3) open a bank account or establish a separate accounting procedure in the new PAC's name. The political action committee may use "PAC" in its name—for example, the National Organization for Women's Political Action Committee (NOW/PAC)—or the PAC reference can be omitted as in Voters for Choice.

For information on establishing PACs for federal races for the offices of president, vice president, United States senator, and United

States representative, contact the Federal Election Commission (FEC) for its excellent pamphlets and guides.[1] In addition, each of the 50 states has its own laws and requirements for contributing funds for state and local office, as well as its own elections agency or commission. If anything, state rules and regulations are less stringent than those of the federal government.

Because federal laws are usually more stringent, an organization that intends to give, or is giving, to both state/local candidates and federal candidates would be better off establishing two separate PACs —one for federal candidates and one for state/local candidates. In most states, for example, an organizational PAC contributing to state races can raise money from the general public as well as from the organization's membership. The same PAC, under federal regulations, could raise money only from members of the organization. With two separate PACs, the federal limitation can be observed for federal races without hampering development of a wider fund-raising market for state and local races.

No group or organization should hesitate to form a PAC because of the legal requirements. The regulations are easy to follow but do require careful management and observance. Since there are legal penalties for failure to comply with these rules, any group starting a PAC would be well advised to first obtain all the necessary information from the FEC or relevant state agency, and, if at all possible, to retain legal or professional counsel.

The fear of many women's groups that forming PACs would jeopardize their nonprofit status is, in most cases, no longer justified. Most women's groups that engage in lobbying for issues are classified by the Internal Revenue Service as 501 (c)4 groups. Included in this classification are NOW, the League of Women Voters, the National Women's Political Caucus, and the American Association of University Women. These are nonprofit groups, so they do not pay income tax, but contributions to them are *not* tax-deductible. Such groups *can* sponsor political action committees.

Some groups have the IRS 501 (c)3 classification. Examples of groups in this class are legal defense funds, foundations such as the Women's Education Fund, the Women's Legal Defense Fund, and the League of Women Voters' Education Fund. This classification means they are nonprofit and contributions to them *are* tax-deductible. Such groups cannot engage in electoral activities and cannot form PACs. However, they can engage in lobbying as long as such activity is within the IRS requirements—e.g., such activity cannot account for more than 20 percent of the group's annual expenditures.

Affiliated vs. Independent PACs

At the federal level, a PAC affiliated with or sponsored by an organization can raise contributions only from the organization's membership. Moreover, all of the PACs of an organization and its affiliates (local branches, chapters, or units) are subject to the same contribution limitations of either $1,000 or $5,000 per candidate per federal race. The upper limit is only for multicandidate PACs—those that contribute to more than six candidates and have been in existence for longer than six months. PACs that are independent of any organization, or "freestanding," can raise money from the general public but have the same contribution limit. Examples of freestanding or independent PACs listed in the resource section of this book are Voters for Choice and the National Committee for an Effective Congress. These freestanding, independent PACs have no sponsoring organization listed. Examples of affiliated PACs are the National Organization for Women's Political Action Committee (NOW/PAC) and the AFL-CIO Committee on Political Education.

A particularly unfair aspect of the modern federal election law resulted from a Supreme Court ruling that an individual candidate can give unlimited sums of money to her/his own campaign.[2] Therefore, one millionaire can give unlimited funds to her/his own campaign for the U.S. Senate, while 250,000 or 1 million members of an organization or union are limited collectively to one contribution of $5,000 to a candidate for each election.

Raising "Soft" and "Hard" Money

Organizations and political parties can utilize "soft money" (money not covered by election agencies' regulations) for some electoral purposes.[3] Soft money is not used for contributions to specific campaigns; rather, it can be used principally for registering voters and for get-out-the-vote (GOTV) activities involving the group's membership or political-party building activities in general. GOTV activities (described more fully in the next chapter) are projects designed to get people to the polls to vote. Organizations can target for GOTV activities their own membership or groups in the general voting population that they think will vote for the candidates these organizations support. As long as these activities are not connected to candidate campaigns, they are not considered electoral contributions and can be paid for by general organizational or corporate funds, as well as by PAC funds.

Such "soft money" expenditures need not be reported to state (in most cases) or federal election agencies. Moreover, "soft money" when used by organizations can come from either 501(c)4 organizational (tax-exempt but nondeductible) funds or 501(c)3 organizational (tax-exempt and deductible) funds. The term *soft money* refers to the belief that these funds are easier to raise since they can come from a variety of sources and can be tax-deductible. Getting non–tax-deductible contributions, for an organization such as NOW or the League of Women Voters, is believed to be more difficult—hence this type of money is referred to as "hard" money. The hardest money to raise is thought to be PAC money because it must be solicited specifically for the purpose of campaig⸱⸱⸱ ⸱ributions or PAC activities, has a very limited tax deductio⸱⸱⸱ ⸱⸱⸱ ⸱d in the amount that can be contributed, and mus⸱ ⸱⸱⸱ the election agencies.

Having raise⸱ ⸱⸱⸱ I believe soft money is actually hardest to r⸱ ⸱⸱⸱ses, particularly if you want funds with no st⸱⸱⸱ ⸱ experience, the easiest money to raise is smal⸱ ⸱⸱orm of memberships and contributions (har⸱ ⸱⸱ ⸱t organizations. PAC money falls between h⸱ ⸱⸱ ⸱money in terms of difficulty. True, it must be ⸱⸱⸱ ⸱st be received in small amounts; but it enables ⸱⸱⸱ to become involved in electoral activity. The difficul-⸱ ⸱ PAC money are that (1) many people have lost faith ⸱ ⸱ candidates and the election process; (2) they feel there are ⸱ ⸱ choices; and (3) some people would rather give to the candi-da⸱ directly.

Yet, there are many people who would rather give to an organizational PAC than directly to the candidate, because PACs can do the research work that they cannot do on their own to determine which candidate supports their issues and is viable. Moreover, PACs represents organized interests such as women's rights, which many individuals may share, but if one's contributions are given individually, one's cause may go unrecognized.

What Is an Independent Expenditure Campaign?

The independent expenditure campaign is another giant loophole in the current limitations on campaign contributions. When the PAC campaigns for or against a candidate without the candidate's knowledge or permission, the contribution limitations of federal races do not have to be observed. In fact, this type of campaign is currently without an expenditure limitation, but it *must* be independent of the candidate's campaign.

The National Conservative Political Action Committee (NCPAC) is known for "negative" independent expenditure campaigns; in other words, it has conducted campaigns against candidates it is opposed to without supporting any candidate in a race. The intent is to "soften" the targeted candidate for defeat in the race at hand or in an anticipated future race. Negative independent campaigns are frequently controversial because they "take the low road," yet no other candidate in the race can be held responsible for these actions.

Independent expenditure campaigns can also work *for* a candidate's election. The North Carolina Campaign Fund was set up in 1982 for any candidate opposed to Senator Jesse Helms.

Organizations can participate in independent campaigns because they are not *for* any candidate in the race but would like to see one of the candidates defeated. In this manner the organizational PAC does not have to support a candidate, yet can work to defeat a leading opponent.

PACs conducting independent expenditure campaigns either for or against a candidate cannot be in communication with the official campaign. One of the reasons it is easier to conduct a negative independent expenditure campaign is that positive campaigns lend themselves to charges of working with their candidate's campaign and violating spending limitations. But whether the independent PAC campaign is for or against a candidate, if it is separate from the candidate or the official campaign, it can take advantage of a legal loophole for avoiding PAC spending limitations.

Tapping into Existing PACs

For groups or organizations to participate in elections under existing law, the formation of PACs is essential. And for women candidates and women's issues, established women's PACs are perhaps the principal vehicles for providing early campaign money.

Women candidates are caught in a vicious circle: They have traditionally had more difficulty raising early money for campaigns; and they are not taken as seriously because they are without sufficient start-up funds. Not being taken seriously at the beginning can have grave consequences. If the seat that a woman candidate is seeking is an open seat (no incumbent), or if the party believes it has a good chance to win the seat, the woman candidate does not get the endorsement of the party machinery. Frequently women candidates have to fight both a tough primary challenge to win the nomination and then the general race. Although this is changing, both the Democratic and Republican parties have been slow to recruit women and slot them for viable races.

PACs organized to promote women candidates and women's-rights issues are rapidly establishing a nationwide network for women to crack the "old boys club." A variety of women's groups are forming PACs. To inquire about obtaining PAC support, contact any of the PACs listed in the Resource Guide.

The largest single network of feminist PACs are NOW/PACs. NOW has set up over 80 PACs at the state and local levels and two national PACs—one for federal races and one for nationally targeted local and state races. NOW/PACs contribute to candidates who support women's-rights issues, both incumbents and newcomers. Increasingly, NOW/PACs are encouraging feminist women to run for office.

The National Women's Political Caucus was established principally to encourage women to run for office. The NWPC has attracted to its ranks professional women politicians who are also interested in women's rights. Decidedly bipartisan, the NWPC has both Republican and Democratic task forces, and although local caucus rules vary, NWPC usually contributes only to females.

NOW, which is composed primarily of feminists who became interested in politics to promote women's issues, does not work as hard at bipartisanship. Many NOW activists consider their "party" to be NOW itself. There are no Democratic or Republican task forces within NOW. NOW/PACs support both Democrats and Republicans, but in 1982 the vast majority of its contributions went to Democrats, simply because they were more supportive of women's-rights issues. Moreover, NOW/PACs are committed to helping Democrats regain control of the U.S. Senate, because the Republican chairmen of Senate committees, such as Hatch and Helms, have been so destructive to women's rights.

Although, proportionately, a large share of NOW/PACs dollars go to female candidates because in the past so few women have run, male candidates for women's rights received more than half of NOW's money. In 1982, when about 20 percent of the candidates for state legislatures were female, NOW/PACs contributed nearly half of its available funds to female candidates. At the federal level, where only 6 percent of the candidates were female, NOW contributed a quarter of its money to women.

Another long-established women's PAC is the Women's Campaign Fund. It contributes only to female congressional and state candidates who are pro–women's rights. This PAC also is bipartisan in philosophy.

PACs sponsored by unions and associations with large female memberships are another source of PAC funds for female candidates.

Today, the teachers' PACs are among the largest and wealthiest. The National Educational Association Political Action Committee was the fifth-largest PAC in the nation in 1982, giving nearly $1.2 million to federal candidates. The NEA is both pro-ERA and pro-choice in reproductive rights, and works closely with national women's groups. Other unions with strong PACs and female constituencies are the Communications Workers of America (CWA), the United Food and Commercial Workers (UFCW), the Amalgamated Clothing and Textile Workers, and the International Ladies Garment Workers.

Two of the fastest-growing women worker's PACs are N-CAP, of the American Nurses Association, and Political Action for Candidate Election for Human Services, of the National Association of Social Workers. N-CAP proudly reminds the public that 1 in 44 American women voters is a nurse. The social workers, frustrated by the Reagan cutbacks in social programs, are increasingly turning to political action. They have already begun their 1984 electoral activity by pledging to register 150,000 new voters, principally their clients. In 1980, they had registered some 20,000 to vote.

PACs are also forming among working women in management. One of the oldest women's groups, the National Federation of Business and Professional Women's Clubs, has formed a PAC and has conducted a political-campaign training seminar in conjunction with its national conference.

Professional women throughout the country are becoming increasingly active in politics and are establishing fund-raising networks. State and local women's unaffiliated campaign funds are being developed in many states and communities. *Business Week* reports that the typical reasons recently given by executive women for forming the PACs are (1) the defeat of the ERA, (2) the desire for increased political clout on women's issues, and (3) the desire for access to political leaders.[4]

Businesswomen's PACs, like their male counterparts, are specializing in larger donations per contributor. The Women's Political Committee in Los Angeles is seeking $2,000 per contributor, and the National Democratic Women's Council of the Democratic National

Committee is requesting $1,000 per contributor.[5]

The trend toward more women's PACs and political fund-raising activity, first noted by the press in 1982, is continuing briskly. I believe it will continue to accelerate, especially when it becomes more obvious that these funds provide real political clout for American women and also the early money needed to launch women's campaigns.

Women's organizations, leaders, and activist members, determined that women will no longer take a back seat in politics, will increasingly put their money to work to change the political scene.

A Note on the Controversy Surrounding PACs

Some critics argue that PACs are changing the entire nature of the election process. They say that PACs have put Congress on the "auction block"—a rather blunt way of saying that PAC fund-raising makes politicians vulnerable to charges that their votes are for sale to the highest bidder. Bills pending in Congress for PAC reform include provisions for public funding of campaigns for Congress, much like the funds that exist for presidential candidates. Other measures would place further limitations on PAC contributions and on total expenditures allowed for a campaign.[6]

Common Cause, a concerned citizens' group specializing in election-law reform, is conducting a lobbying campaign against PACs and for substantial changes in the election laws.[7] Public concern over the high cost of elections and the growing influence of PACs, plus the Common Cause campaign, has created a climate in which PACs are not popular.[8] The public sees them as the money arm of vested interests who are trying to influence legislators for their own gains. Of the approximately 3,500 PACs today at the federal level, some 1,500 are corporate PACs.

How to Raise Funds—for PACs or Candidates

Fund-raising is like leadership—easy to recognize when successful, but difficult to teach. As with leadership, fund-raising is often a matter of attitude.

When I began fund-raising for organizations, I had the wrong attitude: I hated it, so I simply avoided it. I was secretary-treasurer of the League of Women Voters of Allegheny County in the early 1970s, but I probably did not raise a dime.

During my first years in organizing local NOW chapters, those of us doing the work essentially operated out of our own pockets. Actually, we participated in a kind of barter system. When we went grocery shopping for our families, we bought the supplies, coffee, and cookies for the NOW membership meeting. The people involved paid as they went, either in kind or in small amounts of money. When we gave speeches, we would almost always forget to ask for money, though we always remembered to ask audiences to join us in the next activity.

As our campaigns became more sophisticated and I began to see the growing need for contributions, fund-raising became easier. This is often a major step to easier, guilt-free fund-raising: having immediate goals or programs that require money, and feeling responsible for raising it.

But fund-raising never became exciting to me until October 1981, at NOW's national conference, when we were desperately trying to raise $10 million for the final year of the ERA campaign. People who gave to us could expect nothing personally in return, not even a tax deduction. And by then we had appealed to our own loyal membership time and again. I was giving the keynote address and was ready to announce that we planned to pass the hat yet one more time when one of our senior organizers, Molly Yard, grabbed the mike from my hand and yelled, "Ellie is asking you too gently—the power of the women's movement is on the line! I will match every gift you give equally, and, if I have to, I will give my home to do so!"

In the next hour, as the plastic buckets passed from one row to the next, we raised over $32,000 in cash from a convention of 2,000 of NOW's own hard-core activists. I had never watched anything quite like this, and, frankly, it troubled me that these people who had already given so much were giving yet again.

Later, as I walked through the audience, a delegate stopped me to thank me for the fund-raising effort. I began apologizing to her immediately. "It went on for too long," I explained. "We got carried away."

"No, no," she said. "It was great—the greatest thrill of my life— to take out my checkbook and write a sizable check for *me,* for something I wanted—my rights. I've never done anything like this before in my life without asking my husband or my family. It was for *me*—for what I so desperately want. I felt like an adult."

I was shocked. This was, after all, an activist NOW member. Yet even *we* sometimes don't feel free to spend *for our ideals* without asking permission!

My understanding of fund-raising has changed radically over the years. I now realize that there is no need to feel embarrassed about asking for money. If your cause, campaign, or candidate is to perform a worthwhile community service—to fight for justice, equality, and a decent life—the contributors should thank the campaign for the opportunity to give and to participate. Those of us who are "selling" programs of public works should not apologize. If our campaign (product) is worthwhile and will do all we believe it will do, we are giving the donors the buy of a lifetime. Too often we feel like beggars, but we are not; we are organizers for a better life, and our prices are usually more reasonable than a good dinner on the town.

Yet for the fund-raiser, more than a good attitude is necessary; budgets and goals are also required. Goals should be set somewhat higher than what you actually expect to achieve, but not unrealistically high, or not so high as to have no meaning. The reason is that fund-raising requires positive thinking: Thinking the task is possible helps make it so. You must also have a convincing reason for seeking contributions, one that will persuade people that their contributions are important. Without a compelling "package" to sell, even the best of fund-raisers fall short.

Therefore, before a campaign even begins fund-raising, develop the theory and strategy of the campaign, which will vary depending on whether it's for a candidate, an issue, or a PAC. A PAC strategy, for example, might involve getting more feminist women elected to certain state offices in order to have an impact on a particular issue, such as the Equal Rights Amendment ratification. Another PAC strategy could be built around the defeat of powerful committee chairs who are leading opponents of the group's cause.

Usually the strategy involves a central campaign theme and how the campaign is going to be won. The package is what a fund-raiser sells to the potential contributor, and as such is all-important. Even in the often cynical world of politics, a campaign can't be completely devoid of content. And in the more idealistic world of feminist politics, content—the reason behind any campaign—is absolutely essential.

Also important is the leadership of the campaign, or the candidate. People give to people they believe in; the credibility and personal characteristics of the campaign leaders or the candidates are equally critical.

Once the campaign has begun, the key ingredient of successful fund-raising is asking for contributions again and again. Of course, you might change your appeal each time, but you should return to the same donors and lists of names that have an adequate response rate.

On a second appeal, a fund-raiser might say, "Since you have given already, we felt you would want to know that with an additional amount, we can [do such and such]." Or, "We missed your gift last time, but now we need your help more than ever before." Each additional request can be treated as a campaign report; it gets the potential contributor interested and "vested" in your campaign. The most effective appeal is a direct request. The curious phenomenon of fund-raising is that the more you ask, the more you raise.

How to Do the Asking (and the Thanking)

During my years as NOW president, we raised some $40 million for women's rights—yet I began my fund-raising as a chapter president for NOW with a $464 garage sale at my home in suburban Pittsburgh. Every kind of fund-raising is important, whether it's small-scale or gigantic. In my experience, whatever the sum needed, raising money involves the same basic principles:

1. The leader(s) of the campaign must take a personal interest in it. Complete delegation of the fund-raising task to others simply does not work as well. Donors like to get credit for giving, and they feel particularly rewarded if the leader notices their sacrifice.

2. The development of responsive lists of names, addresses, and phone numbers is the first and basic task of all fund-raising. Professionals can help in this task, and direct-mail lists can be rented and tested, but the most precious lists for fund-raising come from address books and Rolodexes of the campaign's leadership. From this core list, the gathering of names should proceed outward. The campaign might then rent or exchange membership lists of supporting organizations, contribution lists of similar campaigns, and mailing lists of periodical-readers with similar views. More important, the women's-rights community is organized, and computerized lists exist for most of the large organizations in almost every state. Check with the women's organizations listed in the "Resource Guide" for further information.

The list-gathering is limited only by the imagination of the gatherer. All lists, however, must be tested by small sample mailings or phone-banks before the whole list is contacted. If the return rate of the sample is not worth more than the effort, discard the list.

Always begin with lists of people who would most likely be supporters. A fund-raising campaign is not meant to convert hostile audiences but to reach out and tap potential supporters.

3. Requests for funds must be *specific:* Know how much you need and what you are going to do with the money. It is better to have a campaign goal of $267,500 than one that is "around $300,000." Suggest to the contributor an amount appropriate to give.

4. People must be asked *personally* to give, and they must know that the gift is needed. Personalize the requests as much as time and money permit.

5. Giving should be made as easy and painless as possible. Make Mastercard/Visa giving available. Enclose business reply cards. Place a postage stamp on reply envelopes for major donors.

6. Contributors must be thanked. Recognition is important. The more personal the thank-you, the better. Even if you have a personal computer printing the letters, add a personal note if possible. A phone call is great.

7. Spend money on fund-raising. How many times have you heard, "You need money to make money"? Never was this statement more true than in fund-raising. Some campaigns seek to cut their budgets here. Remember, without fund-raising, there is no budget. Cut elsewhere. Of course, fund-raising cannot be "fund-losing"—the costs of fund-raising must be justified by the intake of funds eventually.

8. Create a compelling message. An effective one indicates that the campaign will make a difference and therefore so will the contributor's gift. In election campaigns, the message "We are going to win" is extremely compelling for givers. People do not like to give to a "dead horse." But campaigns that are not expected to win can still send a compelling message in the form of citizens' protest or a promise for the future. For example, many candidates lose once or twice before they gain enough name recognition to win, so the campaign can be viewed as building momentum for a future victory. Or the campaign might be expected to lose by only a small margin, which would weaken the opponent for the next race by proving the incumbent is not invulnerable.

The message of women's PACs is exceedingly popular. Polls show that the public wants more women to run and that women's-rights issues themselves are extremely popular.

How to Stage Events and Receptions

The big trick with events and receptions is to keep costs down while making the affair look expensive and successful. Face the fact that a fund-raising reception to which nobody comes is a disaster; you must always be prepared to "paper" the event—i.e., have plenty of people in attendance, whether or not they paid to come. Free tickets are nice rewards for campaign workers, the press, and appropriate prestigious people who would enhance the event. Of course, the paying guests should be numerous enough to make the event qualify as a fund-raiser, but even worse than losing money is giving the appearance that you have.

To keep costs down, always order for considerably fewer people than you expect, but make sure the food, the decorations, and the site look good.

Selection of the site is extremely important, because the site itself conveys a message. An organizer's axiom is "A smaller room that is full is better than a large room that is half-empty." When in doubt, choose a room that can be made larger or smaller as the event demands.

Comparison-shop every aspect of the event. Invitations should be professionally done by a union printer (important at all times, but especially so with campaigns), but the costs can be lowered by some competitive bidding.

The basic ingredient of a successful fund-raising event is a high-quality guest list. Use lists that are known producers and have recently been "cleaned" (had any bad addresses corrected or deleted). And don't limit your use of the list to the sending of invitations—an event's success can be almost directly measured by the number of follow-up calls made. Putting an invitation or solicitation in the mail for an event is only the first step. The second step involves calling everyone on the list and "selling" them on the event. These should be personal phone calls, preferably made by people who know the invitees or by campaign workers who are able to sell on the phone.

Large or small, some of the most successful events are held at the homes of well-known contributors or supporters. The best homes to use are generally those that are the easiest for guests to find; out-of-the-way locations usually cut down attendance. Frequently, however, the home and/or the well-known contributor brings out the crowd. How do you get a well-known supporter to offer the use of his or her home for an event? Again, *asking* is key. People love to help if they know what they can do. If you're not sure the person is a supporter, ask. If your campaign is popular, people will want to contribute their homes, their restaurants' catering, their printing, and so forth. Remember you are offering them a grand opportunity to help and to reach many people while they are doing so.

Such in-kind contributions are as good as cash: The more that is donated, the larger the net proceeds of the fund-raising event.

Direct Mail

Direct mail, or the mailing of letters of solicitation for contributions, is as much a form of advertising as it is fund-raising. With direct mail, you reach into the home or office of a potential supporter. Even if direct mail breaks even or loses money for the campaign, it accomplishes two objectives: (1) It reaches a wide audience with the campaign's message; and (2) it helps to create, from the replies, the "golden" lists of supporters that can be solicited time and time again.

Direct mail is a natural fund-raising tool for women's organizations and for female candidates. Women respond more to mail, and although they don't have as much money as men do, they are willing contributors of smaller gifts. (The average gift in response to direct mail fluctuates between $16 and $25.) Moreover, women's mailing lists tend to be very useful politically. According to direct-mail consultant Roger Craver, "a majority—and often a *substantial* majority —of the donors to public interest groups, political committees, and candidates are women. I expect this proportion will increase as women become more politicized and as more women enter the work force."

To be most helpful in a campaign, direct mail must be started early. One or even two years early is appropriate for major races. A successful program begins with testing: first the "package"—the carrier envelope, the letter, the return device, and the business reply envelope; then the lists to which the package is mailed; and then random samplings of 2,000–3,000 names from larger lists. If the test results meet the campaign's objective, then the direct-mail package is "rolled out" to the whole list. The whole process can take several months, partly because direct mail sent at bulk postage rates can take up to three weeks for delivery, especially if sent nationwide.

This is an expensive form of fund-raising—an average direct-mail package, including postage, costs some 20–30 cents. But for women's-rights issue and for feminist candidates—given that so much work has already been done to develop the lists—and for issues and candidates that depend on a great many small gifts, direct mail is an ideal method of fund-raising. According to Roger Craver, "Little gifts come with no strings attached. Don't become dependent on big contributors. The small contributor has faith in the organization setting the agenda— the big contributor often wants to have a special influence."

Direct mail has many different purposes. Sometimes it is intended only to build lists for later fund-raising appeals—a strategy called "cold prospecting" for "golden or house lists." Sometimes "cold prospecting" is planned to be mailed at a net loss in order to build a large house list. If a loss does occur, the campaign will make up the difference, and then some, when it mails repeated appeals to the golden list. Representative Barney Frank's campaign was so strong that in its final months he was mailing to his house list nearly every thirty days. Frank (D-MA) raised more money ($1.5 million) than any other candidate for the House in 1982. NOW's ERA countdown campaign was so successful in its final months that we raised several hundred thousand dollars a month by mailing to our house list every six weeks.

Sometimes direct mail can be a campaign advantage whether it makes a net profit or loses money. It can establish a large cash flow and thereby demonstrate that the candidate or the PAC is capable of raising money and has popular appeal to large numbers of small donors. When Representative Elizabeth Holtzman ran for the U.S. Senate from New York, many thought she could not raise the money; yet her direct mail established her as very popular with a national audience. Once she reversed the conventional wisdom that she could not raise money, she attracted, of course, more money. She went on to win the primary from an initially better-funded candidate, Bess Myerson.

How should a direct-mail campaign be orchestrated? Here are some practical tips that could make the difference:

- Hire a top-notch direct-mail consultant. Years of testing and experience have taught the professionals the dos and don'ts, chief of which is: Don't experiment on yourself. Small errors result in big losses. For example, listing the contribution options on the return card in a downward sequence—"Please give $100, $50, $25, $15, $10, or $———"—is not as effective as "Please give $10, $15, $25, $50, $100, or $———." Escalating the dollar amounts influences the potential donor to give higher amounts.

  Find consultants through political professionals, campaign recommendations, political parties, or organizations you trust, and always check the references of any consultant. The very hiring of a top-flight consultant signals that you mean business. If you can't afford his or her fee, negotiate. (You *can* afford the testing to tell you if direct-mail fund-raising will work for your campaign.)
- The creativity of the direct-mail package can make or break the appeal. The writer of the package's material must state the campaign message in a compelling way.

- Don't confuse the reader with too many messages—stick to one compelling message or, at most, two. Don't ask the reader to do anything other than contribute. If you *must* make another request, remember that each added request (such as filling in a questionnaire) depresses the percentage of contributions returned.
- Postscripts are important—add one. After the salutation and opening lines, the *P.S.* is probably the next most widely read part of a letter. Make it a reminder to contribute, or an incentive to act.
- Make sure the person who signs the letter is credible to the audience. Of course, it helps if the signer is known to a large audience, as a movie star, say, would be, but credibility on the issue is essential. A well-known person who is not credible on the issue is not the ideal signer.
- The lists should be the best you can create, rent, or obtain through exchange. They are a crucial part of the success or failure of the direct-mail campaign.

Phonebanks and Canvassing

The sophisticated term for soliciting contributions by phone is *telecommunications marketing.* Whatever it's called, phonebanking works.

The personal touch of a phone call can provide the extra push to move a person from just thinking about a campaign to becoming an active contributor. Phonebanks are staffed by volunteer or paid campaign workers (attendance is usually more regular if the workers are paid), using a script. They do not read the script word for word, but they do cover it point by point. For major contributions, phoning is also very effective if done by the PAC leaders or by the candidate.

A good-size phonebank has between 10 and 20 telephoners. Phonebanks generally operate from 5:00 P.M. to 10:00 P.M., Sunday through Thursday. As with direct mail, the primary sources here are lists of organizations and supporters. Phonebanking generally continues throughout the campaign as long as there are phone callers and profitable lists to call. When all lists are completed, start them over again as long as response is profitable. If a mailing goes to these lists before the calling begins, it makes the job easier. *Duplication is excellent and important in fund-raising.* A person may not respond to the first request, but may eventually respond.

Asking, and asking again, is critical. It begins to create a bandwagon effect: "This campaign must be important. People are calling me on it—writing to me about it. I'm seeing it in the newspapers and on TV. I'd better pay attention."

Preparation of lists from which to call is a basic necessity. There should be at least one paid coordinator to prepare lists and to make sure invoices (plus a preprinted thank-you note and a return envelope) for the contributions go out immediately after the call has been made. There's no sense in soliciting the pledge if the follow-through is not instantaneous.

Canvassing door to door for campaign dollars is more difficult than phoning. At the door, the size of the gift is usually smaller than over the phone, but total contributions can be considerable. The NWPC has raised from $10,000 to $42,000 a month through this type of canvassing; and Representative Toby Moffett (D-CT), in his unsuccessful challenge of Senator Weicker (R-CT) in 1982, told me he raised $10,000 a week through door-to-door canvassing.

In canvassing for contributions, paid workers are normally more dependable. Neighborhoods, instead of lists, must be carefully chosen.

Product "Sales"

Affluent campaigns can afford to give away such things as buttons, bumper stickers, and insignia jewelry, but many organizations and campaigns raise significant amounts of money through sales of these items. Indeed, all kinds of sales—garage sales, bake sales, art sales, greeting-card sales, auctions, sales of ads in program books and sales of campaign or cause-related buttons, bumper stickers, T-shirts, and insignia jewelry—can be categorized as "product sales." I use the word *sales* with the warning that unless donors are asked to make a contribution for these items, the campaign may have to pay sales taxes.

When I first began fund-raising, sales were a popular way to raise money at the local level. Garage sales were especially popular. Members or supporters willingly gave major items and, amazingly, just about everything sold. We would collect the items over a long period of time; advertise the function primarily with flyers and home-made street signs; and use the supporter's house whose garage, driveway, and location were best suited to such a sale. A bake sale can always be coupled with a garage sale. Although bake sales seem out of fashion and their proceeds rather small, they do work. All proceeds from such sales are profit, since the location, materials, and labor are donated.

Well-organized sales can readily collect $500 and up.

Art sales and auctions work on the same principle as garage and bake sales: All materials are donated, thus all the proceeds are profit. "Celebrity" auctions, currently in vogue in feminist fund-raising, provide an evening's entertainment and remarkable fund-raising opportunities. Items are donated by both well-known people and ordinary people supporting the campaign. A well-known person can contribute almost anything and it will sell—especially if it's autographed. Items from an average supporter must have more intrinsic value.[9] Normally posters and items of artistic or historical value do well. Such events can provide a very entertaining evening, especially if the items are interesting, the auctioneers lively, and the bidding good-natured yet competitive. People generally enjoy auctions, which makes the "giving" painless. It's not unusual for such auctions to gross several thousand dollars.

Sales of buttons, bumper stickers, T-shirts, and insignia jewelry can also add up. My first effort at such sales was a feminist women's necklace our local chapter bought for 75 cents and "sold" for contributions of $4.25 each. In a short time we earned over $750 on this novelty item, which you could buy nowhere else. But I noticed something else in the sales. There was another factor that made our return on investment even greater.

Buttons, insignia jewelry, T-shirts—all can carry a message. Supporters love to wear them, so it makes fund-raising fun and at the same time serves as a form of advertisement. To be profitable, the price must be set considerably higher than the cost. But even though people know the price is inflated, they will gladly pay it so they can make a contribution and receive something that advertises their support. What's more, in paying for these items, people will value them more and wear them for a longer period of time than if you simply give such things away.

Products like insignia jewelry can also be used as incentives in direct mail to raise the level of giving. With a contribution of $25 or more, offer the giver a special pin commemorating the campaign. Many contributors love such incentives, and the campaign receives higher-than-average contributions *and* "walking advertisements."

I've become a strong believer in product sales. Yet many condemn such activities as too penny-ante in comparison with big-time fund-raising. Critics also label this type of fund-raising "typically female."

Such criticism not only is sexist but also overlooks both the fund-raising and the organizing value of product sales. They require very little up-front money and allow many people to join in. Moreover, they provide an outlet for supporters who cannot otherwise be active in the campaign. Fund-raising that's fun and involves a lot of people is a rare opportunity. Besides, such fund-raising does not necessarily mean modest proceeds. Millions of dollars have been raised by these "sales." Such events usually are small initially, but when the skills are perfected, the revenues grow bigger and bigger. The first significant national ERA fund-raiser I commissioned was selling a medallion necklace commemorating the bicentennial. We netted $75,000 on this piece of jewelry. Yet I would never have had the nerve to take on this project without that first necklace that netted $750.

I have a motto about fund-raising: It all counts. Organizing it (and organizing in general) is like preparing a spaghetti dinner (another tried-and-true fund-raiser) for company: The recipe is the same whether you're serving many people or a few. For many, you just throw in another pound of spaghetti and make more sauce. Once you have the recipe down, it's easy to increase it. My "another pound of spaghetti theory" is that bigger is not necessarily more complicated or more difficult.

Allocating the Campaign Treasury for Candidates

Budgets are goals. Although they are subject to constant revision and adjustment as the campaign develops and changes, the fact is that without a budget the campaign has no roadmaps or measure of its financial progress.

Functional budgets are the easiest kind to understand, develop, and live by for the duration of a campaign. Their basic format involves three steps. First, starting from Election Day and working backward, specify in detail the cost of all the jobs, services, and activities you require. Second, carefully estimate cash receipts from your fund-raising program. Third, prepare a cash-flow schedule of projected receipts and expenditures to accompany the functional budget.[10] By following these three steps, you will obtain the essentials for your financial planning.

In drawing up the budget, remember these two points in particular: (1) The first funds needed are the seed money for fund-raising itself; and (2) cutting corners too sharply in fund-raising will result in a smaller treasury for the entire campaign.

Remember, too, that although modern campaign budgets rely heavily on media advertising and less on get-out-the-vote activities, *both* are essential. The importance of GOTV activity is frequently underestimated. Media expenses tend to increase as the election date draws near, primarily during the last month (except for production and development). GOTV operations are inexpensive by comparison, although they do require funds over a longer period of time.

There are many excellent inexpensive guides to campaign finances and management. Also, both the Democrats and the Republicans conduct training sessions for candidates and campaign workers, as do the key women's-rights organizations. The Women's Education Fund, which began as an arm of the National Women's Political Caucus, frequently conducts nationwide seminars for candidates, campaign managers, and key campaign workers. Both the National Organization for Women and the National Women's Political Caucus conduct workshops and training sessions, primarily for their memberships. All of these training seminars are relatively inexpensive. See the resource section of this book for further information.

Allocating PAC Support to Candidates

The most difficult question PACs confront is which candidates to endorse and/or support. The choice is a fundamental policy decision of the PAC and must be made by its decision-makers in accordance with the special mandate, philosophy, and goals of the PAC. There is, however, one basic principle to be applied when allocating PAC support: PACs must spend some of their resources on research and reconnaissance. Without information independently gathered, a PAC may make embarrassing mistakes in its choices of candidates.

Frequently PACs and organizations rely on questionnaires that they develop and provide to candidates to obtain information on their positions. Let's face it—candidates know how to tell a group what it wants to hear, even without resorting to lying. (And a few just lie.)

Questionnaires can also create political gaffes. An incumbent candidate who has been the group's strongest ally—to the extent, perhaps, of sponsoring key favorable legislation—will see red on receiving a questionnaire asking her or his position on this legislation. "Don't these people know I've been working for this legislation? How insensitive [read "ungrateful"] can they be?"

PACs should know their friends; they deserve your support because of their records. Long, involved questionnaires can be considered a form of harassment by a busy campaign staff. Certainly they win no friends—and frequently engender resentment, particularly when a little independent research can provide much more adequate answers.

Before entering a race to support or endorse, a PAC should determine independently (from several sources):

1. The candidates' positions.
2. The viability of the campaign—i.e., the difficulty of the election.
3. What other groups are doing in this race. Discovering that your allies have taken the opposite position from the one you are considering might affect your decision.
4. The importance of the race in terms of the political clout of the incumbent, or the clout of the position itself.
5. How and to what extent this race furthers the goals of the PAC.

The PAC must defend its political contributions and decisions to its donors. The PAC might make a mistake on a race, especially if it is supporting numerous candidates, but it should not make such a mistake because of inadequate research. If it does, it will eventually lose credibility with its contributors.

When there are candidates to support and campaigns to run, money is the essential ingredient. But if there are too few candidates to support, recruiting candidates becomes the issue. For women, the lack of adequate campaign money has also been a major problem in candidate recruitment. Having examined fund-raising, let's turn to the candidates and find out what's blocking women from running, what to consider in deciding to run, and some tips for the election campaigns.

Women on the Ballot—And in Office

The best way to assure recognition of women's political concerns is to elect more officeholders who not only are pro–women's issues but are women themselves. Women should think seriously about running for office and encourage other women to do so. The quickest way for us to elect more women to public office is for more women to run as candidates. Running for office requires enormous drive, determination, and an understanding of the realities of getting elected. But it is also easier than you might think. Here are some basic considerations that might help you decide.

First Step: Forget the Myths of Why Women Shouldn't Run

Years ago, when I was in graduate school studying political science, I considered writing a paper on how to run for public office. It was a case of bad timing: There was so little information on the subject back then that I had to switch to another topic.

Today, information abounds, and there are even manuals on how women can run for office—things that were unheard of in the 1960s. Yet this knowledge, so essential in any democracy, is still not as widespread as some of the old myths—especially those designed to discourage women from running for public office. For example:

MYTH: Women are their own worst enemy.
REALITY: Contrary to popular assumption, being a female is an advantage to a candidate, not a disadvantage.

Today, most women candidates enjoy their biggest boost from women voters at the polls. Indeed, Republicans feel that one way to close the gender gap against Ronald Reagan is to put more women on the Republican ticket so they will pull votes in his direction. Until recently, however, most people would have thought this not to be the case.

In 1971, I codirected an extensive study of the attitudes of 1,000

Pittsburgh women—both Democrats and Republicans—toward women candidates.[1] Even after all these years, some of the interviews are still vivid in my memory, and so are the general insights we gained. These interviews completely erased for me the stereotypical notion that women are female candidates' toughest critics.

A startling 80 percent of the women I surveyed wanted more women to run because (1) electing more women would advance the status of women in politics and would help society, (2) women provided superior qualifications for office, and (3) women were as qualified as men to hold office. The small minority of women who were opposed to electing more women to office felt that (1) politics was a man's world and women belonged at home, and (2) men were more qualified.

We found not only that most women felt women would do as good a job as men once in office, but, more important, that while some felt women would do a worse job, twice as many (18.2 percent) felt women officeholders would do a *better job*.[2] The findings pointed clearly to the possibility of a women's voting bloc emerging in the future.

Today, polls reveal that women enjoy even higher levels of support from women than they did in the early 1970s. But is there enough support to elect a woman president?

Pollsters generally agree that this question is a poor measure of female candidates' support levels, because it is the most extreme question. Polls consistently show higher support for women running for lesser offices than for a woman running for president. Compare the situation of Catholics in 1960. Catholics held all kinds of public offices before John F. Kennedy broke the Catholics-can't-be-president barrier. Once one Catholic became president, even though the election was extremely close, the issue of whether a Catholic was electable as president vanished.

Until we elect the first female president, the question of whether a woman can be elected president will remain. However, it can hardly be used as a barometer of support levels for women in politics, even though today (according to a Virginia Slims 1980 poll) a majority of both women and men would support a "qualified" woman for president (78 percent of women and 69 percent of men—once again, the gender gap).[3]

When individual races are analyzed at the state and local levels, women's advantage can be clearly seen. State races involving a woman candidate reveal a gender gap in favor of the woman candidate, meaning that more women than men tend to support her. The gap can be as large as 10–15 percent. When voters are asked, "Would you be more likely or less likely to support the candidate because she is female?" both men and women are more likely to support her *because* she is a female, with women voters more positive than men. Although there is a gender gap, both men and women are more supportive of women candidates today.[4]

MYTH: Female candidates don't win as often as men.

Some observers point to the fact that there are fewer women in public office and conclude that women don't do as well as men in elections.

The post–1982 election news coverage reported women had difficulty winning, pointing to several statewide races women lost and to the seemingly low percentage of women candidates (32 percent) who won in congressional bids.

REALITY: Fortunately, these are not accurate measures. In 1982 only two women ran for governor and two for the U.S. Senate. These numbers are so small that percentages are meaningless.

As for House races, many of the women running belonged to the minority party in their districts—in other words, they ran against incumbents in congressional seats that were safe for the incumbents. Republican Bonnie Hicky (daughter of a local Republican politician) ran against Congressman Dan Rostenkowski (D-IL), the powerful chairman of the House Ways and Means Committee, in a safe seat in the center of Chicago's large North Side Polish neighborhood—over 70 percent Democratic. This type of candidate is considered a "sacrificial lamb," with no chance of winning. If such races are eliminated from the congressional calculations, as well as races in which women ran against other women candidates, the batting average for women goes up over 50 percent. When you consider that congressional seats are more expensive and difficult to win, the average is encouraging.

Winning at the polls is not the problem for women. The problem is that *not enough women are running*. Frequently, the party establishment opposes the woman candidate—she is simply not in the right club to get the nod from party leaders for nomination. It is just another form of job discrimination that women face. A woman, after all, may not look like a senator, therefore the powers that be do not think of her as a possible senator. Even tougher than the problems of image is the fact that women candidates frequently have to face both a contested primary challenge and a contested general election in order to win. (The most notable exception occurs when an elected official who dies in office leaves a widow who becomes the establishment's nominee.)

MYTH: A woman should run as a qualified candidate, not as a woman.
REALITY: Given the small number of women in office, especially in state and federal seats, the fact that the candidate is a woman will most likely be an issue. Whether the candidate brings up the issue or somebody else does, it will become an issue. Since voters want more women in public office, in my opinion a woman's gender is one of the assets of her campaign.

By ignoring the issue, the woman candidate risks taking for granted the constituency of women and men who want more women in office. Like any constituency, these voters want to know that their candidate is responsive to them. Of course, any candidate must make appeals to a broad spectrum of voters; but she cannot afford to forget her female base of support. Moreover, a female candidate who addresses the fact that she's female in a positive manner—for example, by suggesting that she will bring a fresh perspective to office—will be more effective at earning the support of women's organizations.

MYTH: A female political candidate has to be a lawyer or significantly more qualified than her male counterpart to run.
REALITY: About half of all female officeholders have employment backgrounds in traditionally "female" jobs like teaching, nursing, and social work. Although as many elected women as men have graduated from college, fewer women have gone to graduate or professional schools. Women's experiences in organizations and in women's jobs are acceptable to the electorate. Moreover, women officeholders, before being elected, have actually had more experience in appointive public office than have men.[5]

MYTH: A woman should not run against a woman.
REALITY: No one would even imagine saying this to a man.

MYTH: Women can't take losing.
REALITY: When someone says, "Politics is too competitive for women," the real message is "Don't run—you might lose."

Of course, if you don't run, you *surely* won't win.[6]

A recent study reveals that women officeholders are actually somewhat more ambitious than their male counterparts. A majority of women at every office level intend to seek other offices in the future. The numbers are astounding: 76 percent of female state legislators, as compared to 62 percent of the males; 80 percent of the female local council members, as compared to 72 percent of the males.[7]

MYTH: One woman on the ticket is enough. Another will only divide the vote.

REALITY: This is another variation of the "don't run" theme. In 1982, two women wanted to run for the three at-large county commissioner seats in Alachua County, Florida. They were told, "Don't run—you'll divide the votes for women, and all the men will win." Both women ran anyway—and they *both* won.

These seven myths and a million other reasons are given to discourage women from running for office. Ignore them and proceed on your election agenda.

Second Step: Plan Ahead—Invest in Your Political Future

Women interested in public office should plan ahead and "get involved." The best way to do this is by following the lead of officeholders who gained their experience working in other candidates' political campaigns and for political parties. Women have an additional avenue —working for women's PACs and organizations, many of which are listed in the resource section of this book.

Frequently, women work for campaigns, parties, and/or organizations without an eye to the future and without recognizing the value of their work or requiring adequate recognition for it. The traditional work for women in campaigns is canvassing (going door to door), phonebanking, mailings, and organizing the details of fund-raising events. These are essential operations to any campaign and are valuable skills to acquire. But so are the campaign jobs that are not traditionally female: field director, press secretary, advance person, campaign manager. All of these positions involve you in work that puts you closer to the candidate, and these are the campaign aides most often rewarded with jobs if the candidate wins, or with recommendations for other campaigns or political work.

A good entry into political campaigns is a background in organization work.[8] Women's organizations are often a valuable source of learning and encouragement for future political careers. Organizations are in need of writers, public-relations people, fund-raisers, project managers, event and conference workers and planners, issue specialists, researchers, and so on. Often, hardworking, competent people are promoted rapidly through the ranks in political organizations, including political parties. Jobs in political organizations, including women's PACs, do not pay well, if at all; hence the constant scramble for good people. But the experience is invaluable.

Political-campaign jobs are notoriously low-paying, with plenty of stress and little sleep. Key political-campaign personnel tend to be young (25–35) white males who use the jobs as stepping-stones into political careers. It is not unusual to see the young men paid while more-experienced older women are volunteering. The young men's jobs usually have more impressive titles and they are viewed as professionals—after all, they are being paid. Thus, the best way to get ahead and be taken more seriously in campaign work is by obtaining one of the paying jobs.

A good way of learning the ropes in politics is by doing—by being involved. But it is easier if you have some training and preparation for the work.

Take time to learn not only about public policymaking in areas you care about, but also about the process of lawmaking. For example, often people who are interested in women's rights will first learn about sex discrimination, and then—more willingly—about the governmental processes for eliminating it. Knowledge of the process of government is fundamental. For the federal level, *Congressional Quarterly* material is excellent. The League of Women Voters can provide material at the local or state level. When in doubt, go directly to the government agency in which you are interested; you should become accustomed to going to the primary source for any information you need.

If you would rather learn about politics and campaigns in a group, many organizations hold conferences and workshops on politics and campaigns, and both political parties hold candidate training sessions throughout the country. These various "training academies" are reviewed in the resource section. Don't be shy about attending such conferences or workshops. You don't need to know somebody to attend. Many women go alone, and there is always a first time.

A Note on Where to Start

There is no one path to public office. Candidates are not required to have special preparation, and they do not have to be in politics to decide to run. As in any other field, entry at the top can come most easily from being at the top in some other field. Increasingly, people in careers with visibility (radio, TV, the space program, etc.) and people who are successful in business or other organizations run for office and win. Many young people—mid-to-late twenties—with little experience win at the local and state level. They became involved, decided to run—and won. Winning isn't essential the first time. Frequently the first election challenge is a step toward making victory possible the second or third time.

Third Step: Deciding When to Run

For women, the decision to run for office usually follows an involvement in organizations, campaigns, or an issue. Today, many women are deciding to run at a later age than men. However, the earlier in life a woman decides, the easier it is to take the necessary steps to prepare for it. Now that more women are making career and work decisions earlier, more undoubtedly will make political decisions earlier.

For women who have families, the decision seems harder. It doesn't have to be. Many women worry that it is nearly impossible to combine family responsibilities and public careers, particularly because politics does not have regular work hours. Yet polls show that most male officeholders (70 percent) but less than half (49 percent) of women in elected office thought political activity negatively affected their family relations.[9] Women may implicitly know that, unlike many careers, politics can involve the whole family.

Actually, I have found that involving one's spouse and children in the political work minimizes the alienation. I was involved in public and organizational work—albeit not traditional politics—during most of the years my children were growing up, and both my husband and I noticed that the more involved I became, the better our children did in school. They would ask me how I knew so much about an issue on which I had given a speech, or where I learned so much that I could testify before a legislative committee. While some families go on picnics or vacations to grow closer, ours went to demonstrations, conventions, congressional hearings, and marches.

Spouses of female officeholders are more likely to encourage and support their work than are spouses of male officeholders (67 percent to 44 percent, according to the Eagleton study).[10] Married women active in organizations and politics tend to have supportive husbands, proud of their wives' work. Of course, one of the reasons why there are so few women in public office may be that husbands fearful of the family impact talk their wives out of running. I have found that husbands' attitudes are definitely a major consideration for women considering running. Clearly, the more women role models there are that combine politics and family, the quicker this issue will be resolved.

Fourth Step: Choosing the Seat

Wanting to run, preparing yourself to run, and deciding when to run
are all prerequisites to the most important decision a politician can
make: choosing the "seat" or office to run for. Decisions of timing and
electability are crucial—but most important, the seat must be "winna-
ble." To determine whether it is, you must look at the numbers of the
race and answer a series of questions concerning the seat.

- Is there an incumbent who will be seeking reelection? If so, analyze
  the vulnerability of the incumbent. By how large a percentage has
  the incumbent won in the past? What are the reputation, resources,
  support level, and constituencies of the incumbent?
- What is the electoral history of the seat? What party has held the
  seat—which years, by what margins? What is the political-party
  makeup of the electorate? What are their religious affiliations, occupations, income levels, and racial and ethnic composition?
- If there is no incumbent, is there likely to be another challenger in
  the primary as well as in the general election? Assess the challenger's
  strengths and weaknesses—e.g., his/her name recognition, resources, group support. Is there a way to preempt the field in your
  party so you will not have a primary race? If you have a primary
  race, will the general election be easier?
- How much will it cost to try to win the seat? You can estimate the
  cost of both the primary and general elections by finding out what
  the cost has been in the past two elections. State and federal election
  agencies have the campaign reports of contributions and expenses
  for the past elections. An alternate source of such data is newspaper
  reports, or try to interview people politically knowledgeable about
  the area.

Generally, incumbents win elections. Less than 10 percent of all
congressional candidates are defeated, usually, in any given election
year. In 1982, only 8 percent of all congressional incumbents were
defeated. The same "rule of incumbency" works, probably to an even
greater degree, for local legislative districts because most seats are
considered safe for an incumbent of the majority party in that election
district. This is not accidental: The legislative and congressional district lines are "gerrymandered"—unfairly drawn—to favor the party
of the incumbent.

To account for shifts in the population, the state legislature redraws
political district lines for Congress and the state legislature every ten

years, after the decennial census is taken. This redistricting process is meant to assure every citizen a vote of equal weight under the "one person, one vote" rule. Because it is done in a political arena and helps to determine who will win the seat and what party will win the balance of power, redistricting is one of the most important political decisions of each decade. Candidates running for state legislative seats or congressional seats should ask themselves, "For whom, if anybody, was the seat created?"

Fifth Step: Plan Ahead for Support and Endorsements

Although women candidates have distinct advantages, they are also more prone than men to a number of pitfalls, particularly in finding financial support for running.

Women candidates have had a difficult time raising "early" money and funds for the final three weeks of the election.

The early money is difficult to raise because when a woman announces her intentions to run, too many people are quick to discount her candidacy. Since women are commonly regarded as easy entrants to beat, other candidates—usually men—are encouraged to enter the race. While an announcement usually solidifies support, for a woman it often intensifies the debate over who would make the best "real" candidate.

Thus, a woman must declare as early as possible and with as large a treasury and as many endorsements as possible to preempt the field. It is essential for women to give a very early signal that they are playing "hardball."

Money spent in the last days of a race is as important as money raised in the initial days. No matter how much is spent on the campaign, enough must be saved for the last-minute blitz of advertising and promoting your candidacy. Voters have short memories—the last candidate they hear from is frequently the one who gets their votes.

Republican women (and men) can obtain more party financial support than Democratic women (and men), because Republicans traditionally have more money to spend. In 1982, Democratic party congressional committees were outspent by Republican committees seven to one. Thus, Democratic women are more dependent upon women's organizations to help them. Organizations, especially women's groups, have been more supportive (two to one) of Democratic than Republican women.[11]

Women's groups can be very supportive, but they can also be very harsh on a woman candidate who has not supported *them,* even though the candidate supports their issues. These organizations have higher expectations of a female candidate and don't want to be "used" by a woman who will not help other women get ahead. You should therefore never take the support of these organizations for granted. They should be contacted early—before you publicly announce your candidacy—and a good relationship should be established.

Your rewards will be severalfold. Volunteers, funds, and expertise will be made available. These organizations want to help women candidates—but, like the candidate herself, they want to be taken seriously. They want access to the candidate and her campaign, and they also want their work to be recognized by the candidate. A female candidate who approaches these groups with respect and camaraderie will be surprised at the high level of support she receives from volunteer help in obtaining financial backing, guidance, and influence among the electorate. Moreover, if she takes pride in the support of women's organizations, rather than treating them as somewhat embarrassing distant relatives, she will pick up points and admiration.

For female candidates who are not on the inner track in establishment party politics, support from women's organizations can be critical. But for all types of female candidates who support women's issues, women's organizations can in turn provide a base of support. Although neither men nor women obtain most of their support from organizations, more elected women list organization support as having been extremely helpful for their victories.

Sixth Step: Estimating Resources

Once you have determined that an office can be won, you have to make realistic assessments of your financial resources and your candidacy's assets and liabilities. This information will be as crucial as the earlier review of polling data concerning the likely challengers: Knowing your resources will help you determine the strategy of your race.

When estimating financial resources, you must begin with yourself. Few people want to invest in a campaign that the candidate does not want to invest in. If the candidate is not willing to take any realistic financial risk, few others will be willing to do so. Running for office is like starting a business: Investors expect the entrepreneur to guarantee the initial loans. It does no good to play it safe at this point. In the final analysis, the candidate is investing in her own future.

Very occasionally, a person is so popular and has such a ground swell of public or organizational support that she is drafted to run for office.[12] Only then can the candidate say to supporters, "I'll run if you guarantee me [x amount of dollars] for my campaign treasury." Normally, however, the candidate provides the initial funds. These start-up funds, plus easily obtainable contributions from close associates and friends, must be used to establish the campaign—that is, to provide stationery, phones, and office space, and provide the initial seed money for ongoing fund-raising.

You must develop a financial plan showing how your campaign will obtain adequate funds and how these funds will be spent. If you need $60,000 for a race and can envision raising no more than $10,000, you must think seriously about whether to undertake a project that is clearly beyond your resources.

In making these financial assessments, you must also consider the other assets and liabilities of your candidacy: Who and what groups can you count on for support? What are your strong points—knowledge of issues, experience, platform, name recognition, appearance, and speaking and meeting abilities? In looking at liabilities, the key question is, Can your life stand up to public scrutiny in the areas of finances, work record, and possible scandal? You should draw up a similar balance sheet estimating the resources of your opposition.

In making these assessments, the campaign strategy has to be taken into account. Maybe your campaign will be underfunded, but your opponent has just been involved in a scandal. Or the highly visible issues of the campaign will work to your benefit, but be detrimental to your opponent. Or perhaps you will have more impressive and influential endorsements. Or you may have an unusual get-out-the-vote mechanism.

Seventh Step: Consider Hiring
a Political Consultant

Before making the final decision to run, you should seek out the opinion of professional consultants. Political consultants who specialize in media, fund-raising, and polling can be found in many localities, and particularly in larger cities. If the race is not costly, this step can be omitted; but if the cost of the race exceeds $25,000, professional consultants can save much time, grief, and money in the long run. Most people would not think of making a major investment in anything without consulting experts. Running for political office can also require a major investment, and thus you should check with one or, preferably, more campaign professionals if you are seriously considering entering a race.

Consultants can be located through women's organizations and PACs, through political parties, and through the American Association of Political Consultants. Although many consultants are still not attuned to women's issues, a few now specialize in women candidates.

If the race is statewide or congressional, engage a highly reputed political consultant (or consultants) specializing in media, fund-raising, and public-opinion polling. This signifies the campaign means business. Hiring such a person also attracts more attention and creates greater fund-raising possibilities. Consultants often pay for themselves, because they save time, raise money, and provide a more effective campaign overall.

Most consultants work only on campaigns of candidates who hold similar political philosophies or those of the same political party. Contact them early to check on their availability and to get an estimate of their fees.

Eighth Step: Play for Keeps—Staff a Professional Campaign

A well-run campaign is almost always a prerequisite for victory. And essential to any campaign is a paid, experienced campaign manager. A candidate can't afford to manage her own campaign; successful management of a campaign and effective performance as the candidate will conflict. The candidate's obligation is to look like a winner —appearing fresh and rested—and to use the precious time available for voter contact and campaign appearances, not the sundry details of staffing, finances, and implementing campaign decisions.

Why the emphasis on a *paid* campaign manager? Paid managers will make the campaign their highest priority. Moreover, it's easier to fire an employee than a volunteer, if necessary. The candidate is the manager's boss, but the manager runs the campaign. Other key campaign staff should also be paid if possible—for example, the office manager, receptionist or key clerical staff, and the press secretary. Campaigns constantly need legal advice, and it should be on a professional basis. The keeping of financial records, too, is so important that hiring a professional accountant or retaining a firm with campaign experience is preferable.

Volunteers are also essential, however, and they should be treated as key campaign workers. It takes careful planning and supervision to make the best use of volunteers' time, talents, and experience. Ideally, a paid coordinator is part of the central management of the campaign to ensure that the work of volunteers is tied into the campaign as a whole. Volunteers with experience and time availability should be given responsibilities for projects and supervision.

In campaigns, some people work out and others don't. Frequently, a person who cannot perform one job can be transferred to another with excellent results. However, volunteers whose presence or efforts are definitely counterproductive to the campaign can and should be "fired"; they use phones and office space and can negatively affect the morale of the campaign. On the other hand, if too many volunteers aren't working out, the problem may be with management. Be alert to these problems.

Ninth Step: Use Media
and Polls to Reach Voters

The most expensive items of nearly all political campaigns are public-opinion surveys and the media. A media strategy, whether through paid advertising or public relations, is essential for any-size campaign. Extensive polling is usually reserved for congressional, statewide, or big city races.

The Resource Guide lists several references to campaign guides that include sections on public relations, advertising, and polling, as well as documents available from the Federal Communications Commission on candidate rights. Use them. You cannot afford to "rediscover the wheel" with something as important to your campaign as the media and polling. Mistakes can be very costly.

Effective use of the media sets the tone of your campaign. It builds name recognition and communicates your message to voters whom you otherwise might not be able to reach using traditional door-to-door techniques. I can only begin in these few pages to outline the most important points of planning a media strategy. For small campaigns, common sense and creativity can be your most important assets. For larger campaigns, it pays to use professionals with track records in public relations and political advertising.

To begin, take time to develop your message. Good media coverage of any campaign comes from a substantive campaign strategy. Consider the issues and how you, the candidate, can best put forward your positions. Imagine for a moment what you would consider the best possible media coverage—the best headlines, stories, and news reports on the campaign. Answer these questions: How do you want your campaign to be portrayed in the media? Which issues do you want emphasized? How do you, as the candidate, want to be described by the press? What professional qualifications do you want highlighted? What information about your personal life should be incorporated in stories about you or your family? Are there any special reasons why you decided to run for office? What will you do if elected? All these and more will be asked of you over and over by the media and by voters. Even before announcing, you should know exactly how you want these and other details described to the media and to the public. Once you have clear media goals, it will be easier for you and the press secretary to achieve them.

When using these "press lines" in the campaign, keep the answers short and to the point. Once your message is developed, it is useful to repeat key slogans or campaign themes in brochures, in direct mail, on posters and flyers.

You may want to check with local or national women's groups on the best way to communicate women's-rights issues. For example, the National Abortion Rights Action League, Voters for Choice, and NOW have materials that help candidates discuss the issue of abortion.

Give your campaign a professional look. To reach the media, develop a campaign "kit" that includes favorable press clips (don't forget to secure copyrights), background biographies, issues in the campaign, and possibly background on the staff and on the philosophies of the candidate. This kit also can be used for fund-raising. Within financial limitations, don't cut corners on literature, posters, stationery, advertisements. Campaign colors and logos are an important part of the image you want to project to voters. The overall look of the campaign should not be tacky, but not too slick either. If the campaign looks too cheap, supporters and financial backers won't think you have a chance. On the other hand, if materials are too obviously expensive, it will seem as if you have money to burn and people will think you don't need their help.

Next, you and your top staff must become students of the media. Learn reporters' names and what they cover in *all* the media in your district. A finely tuned newspaper and magazine clipping system should be started as soon as possible. Television and major radio news should be monitored. These are good, substantive tasks for capable volunteers and are critical for a successful media strategy. Make sure the campaign office has TV sets, radios, and newspaper subscriptions. Audio- and videotape players are handy tools for monitoring news and analyzing your performance.

Organize a media team consisting of the press secretary, any experienced PR advisers, and, most important, yourself. The team has two purposes: It is the job of the press secretary and public-relations advisers to "sell" story ideas; and it is important for them to collaborate on the ideas with others in the campaign. The team members must keep one another informed of outside news. One of the biggest mistakes a campaign can make is to isolate the press operation to one person or one unit and not integrate the media operation into day-to-day campaign planning. The media are very important, and the best minds of the campaign must meet to spend time on press details.

The press secretary should be a ranking member of the campaign, with full access to the campaign decision-makers, and should be heavily involved in scheduling, issue development, and campaign strategies. Given these responsibilities, the press secretary should be an enthusiastic "salesperson" with the skills to screen press calls, build relationships with reporters, and manage an efficient press operation.

However, a press secretary should not be a substitute for the candidate's involvement with the press. You should get to know reporters personally on a face-to-face basis. While president of NOW, I kept a small notebook of reporters' names and phone numbers as a way to track press contacts. At press conferences, it gave me extra confidence to look at the crowd and know many of the faces on a first-name basis. The best and most substantive articles came from reporters with whom we spent time and those to whom we gave in-depth briefings. Whatever the coverage, respect reporters' journalistic integrity. They must maintain a certain level of objectivity and neutrality.

Editorial endorsements by the media can help put a campaign over the top. Most editorial decisions are made public late in the campaign, just before Election Day. Find out early how endorsements are made, who sits on the editorial board, and the background of each member. If necessary, schedule lunches with key editors and put the best possible case forward in person. If you are denied their editorial support, find out whether they will acknowledge a dissenting point of view in the form of an "op-ed" piece or an equal-time television spot made available to opposing candidates.

You should establish certain standards for handling the press. Internally, systems should be set up so that *before* each prearranged media interview, you have some background information on the reporter and a general overview of what will be asked in the interview. You should also know how long the interview will run and the date and time the story will appear. Reporters will often not want to divulge the specific questions they plan to ask, but a good press secretary can elicit a sense of what will be included in the interview. For a broadcast, find out if you are to be interviewed alone or with other guests, who will do the interview, the exact time you are to be at the station, and the exact air time. You should go into an interview knowing these details. Remember, you are reaching thousands, maybe millions of people, and the impressions given to voters through the media are crucial for winning a campaign.

Make sure the campaign's media operation is run efficiently. Press calls should not fall between the cracks. Staff should return press calls promptly and with the information *you are ready to release.* The campaign has no obligation to respond to all queries or to release information when you are not prepared to do so.

If your media budget exceeds $25,000, you should branch out into polling and paid advertising (which go hand in hand). You will need to know how the public perceives your strengths and weaknesses; the level of your name recognition; and public sentiment on the issues you support. Polling will also help you identify the voters you need to win the election, so that you can target your audiences and pinpoint the media you need to reach them.

If the campaign can't afford the full expense of a poll, you may be able to share costs with other compatible candidates, or add questions to another candidate's poll. Again, consult with professionals. Local universities may sponsor research centers capable of doing public-opinion surveys. Or contact the national political parties for recommendations.

As for advertising—a do-it-yourself advertising campaign won't work. Find a good ad agency with whom you have a rapport. Personalities should click, and the creative staff should be on your wavelength.

Television and radio spots are not the place to fool around with used video equipment or homegrown scripts—but spots should not be extravaganzas either. A rule of thumb on costs for production is to estimate spending about 10–15 percent of your total media budget. However, high-priced productions cannot make up for an ill-conceived campaign theme. What you say is as important as how you say it.

Advertising time should be purchased by someone with experience in buying political spots. Agencies get a 15-percent commission directly from the media. Their fee is included in the price you pay for the spots. Some agencies may give the campaign a price break. As with other services, get bids and ask the important fee questions. Media buys should be planned from Election Day backward. Lower rates, availability of spots, and money can dry up closer to Election Day. An experienced time buyer knows the tricks.

Above all, make sure your media advisers know the FCC regulations on candidate access and are familiar with the Fairness Doctrine and personal-attack rules.

The campaign's media strategy is a critical component of modern-day electioneering, and new polling technologies and increased media outlets have drastically changed the rules. Already in use are computer phonebanks, two-way cable interactives, and press conferences by satellite hookup—the opportunities are limited only by money and your imagination. Don't let technology scare you, but beware of too-big dollar signs, and use consultants with a track record.

Tenth Step: Get Out the Vote

Today, campaigns tend to emphasize broad media appeals over the importance of getting-out-the-vote (GOTV) activities. Yet this imbalance can hurt: A candidate may be way ahead in public-opinion polls, but if her supporters don't vote, the polls don't count. Getting your supporters to the polls is the campaign's bottom line.

To do this, supporters must first be identified via polling, canvassing, and phonebanking. On Election Day, GOTV must be followed through by providing transportation to the polls and making last-minute phone calls to remind identified supporters to vote.

Professional consultants often minimize the value of such activity because of the large sums of money required for television, radio, and newspaper advertisement; and because the GOTV aspect of the campaign used to be handled by the political-party apparatus. But party machines are weaker today, and candidates therefore must assemble their own GOTV operations.

GOTV requires a large volunteer "army," because few campaigns can afford to pay all the workers required. This can give female candidates an edge, however, since women are the volunteers of

America, and women's organizations can provide the base of volunteers and coordinators for GOTV activities. While in most elections volunteer activity is devalued, in feminist races it can be an equalizer, counterbalancing vast sums of money spent by opponents.

Many advise that a successful get-out-the-vote campaign target the nonvoters; others think it should target the undecided or those leaning toward their candidate. Yet many still believe they must appeal to the mainstream of voters to win.

I disagree with the notion of taking your own supporters for granted. For over a decade I have watched the New Right organize its minority of supporters and win elections. Segments of the population that are *motivated* to vote win elections. To motivate support, a candidate cannot be "oatmeal," bland, all things to all people. This was fine in the days of party machines, but those days are over. Today, to motivate people to vote, especially through modern media, a candidate must appeal to particular segments of the population. To appeal to everyone is to appeal to no one. I would target first the campaign's supporters, voting and nonvoting, and make sure as many of them as possible actually get out and vote.

Be Flexible: The Most Important Step
You Take Is Often
the One You Can't Plan

Politics, you will discover, is an art, not a science. A campaign is a beehive of constant, fast-paced activity, a model of organized confusion. Formulas and planning are important, but more important is that the campaign take off, that it motivate workers and voters all on the same day—Election Day—to perform at peak levels. It requires organization and motivation—and sometimes the two conflict. A campaign must have spirit, and to build it you sometimes must sacrifice efficiency. For example, the most efficient planning might involve sending a surrogate to a reception, but at the last minute the campaign finds out this will insult an important constituency or a key supporter. Such choices will crop up several times a day, a dozen times a week—hence the nightmare of scheduling. Sometimes the most efficient get-out-the-vote system steps on the toes of key local leaders—or what works in one part of the district conflicts with local customs in another part. Whatever the problem, flexibility enables you to introduce variations quickly. The art of politics requires you to learn the principles and adapt them to particular needs.

The Packaging of the Candidate

Alan Alda portrayed a successful politician in *The Seduction of Joe Tynan.* To this day, Alda has his Joe Tynan suit for public political "performances," such as the speeches he made advocating passage of the Equal Rights Amendment.

Much is known about how a male politician should look. What he should wear. How he should behave. What his wife should do and say. Not so with female candidates. What does a woman senator look like? What does a female gubernatorial candidate wear at a black-tie dinner? Recently, at a black-tie dinner, a female gubernatorial candidate leaned over and said to me, "They think I'm somebody's wife—I don't look like the candidate. Formal dinners are awful for us."

Female candidates must dress in a manner that commands respect, yet does not look characteristically male. They cannot get by with as few outfits as a male candidate, because people expect variety in women's wardrobes and pay close attention to what women candidates are wearing. Women in public positions have commented to me, "They didn't hear my speech because my clothes were wearing *me,*" or "I never feel comfortable. People think I should look softer, but when I do, no one thinks I look like a politician!"

Because women do not have a uniform as men do, the "clothes problem" of a campaign is considerable for a woman. It's a part of sex discrimination, but instead of labeling this as trivial, a campaign should confront it directly and put enough energy and resources into it early in the campaign.

Most women candidates will find that too many items in their wardrobes either do not project authority or are wrong for television. To help you achieve the appropriate "look," here are some tips I've learned painfully:

- Wear solid colors in medium shades—like periwinkle blue, or rose. Avoid prints and checks—they are distracting, especially on television. White and pastels also don't work for either television or public speaking; white fabrics can glare, and too-light pastels look faded. Any color worn should be at least a shade darker than light tan.
- Don't show too much skin. People will not take you seriously if you look more like an entertainer than an officeholder.
- Accept TV makeup whenever it is offered by a program or station. For doing your own campaign spots or making an important appearance on television, hire a professional TV makeup artist if one

is not a part of the deal. This is as important for men as for women. The classic example is the Nixon-Kennedy debates in 1960, which many believe Nixon lost because his "five o'clock shadow" made him appear disheveled and tired. Appearing on television is like being studied through a magnifying glass, but makeup artists can be geniuses at making you look good.

In campaigns, the personal is often political. The candidate's family and/or friends frequently take part in the campaign. A family active in the campaign indicates there is support at home, but the family, as well as the candidate, must understand that they will lose most of their privacy. There is no sense, however, in trying to create a "political" husband in the image of the traditional adoring, supportive, quiet, ever-obedient, helpful political wife. The public won't buy it for men—and one hopes it will soon vanish for women, too. An egalitarian relationship in which each carries his/her own weight is best. And, of course, a husband shouldn't be on his wife's campaign payroll, any more than a wife should be on the payroll of her husband's campaign.

For unmarried candidates, or candidates without family members eligible to campaign, or for candidates who don't want to involve their families, it is possible to separate the private and the public. Frankly, there's a sexist assumption in the current public notion that when you elect a candidate, you are electing a family. This assumption was born in the age when the husband was the candidate/officeholder and his wife was the helpmate: The public got two people to do the job for one salary. Those days are ending—many political wives are employed, more political husbands are employed, and many unmarried candidates are elected. However, if a personal support system is not going to be part of the campaign, a support system must be built into the campaign staff and operations. For example, if family members will not be used as candidate surrogates, then other campaign associates will have to be delegated this task.

I don't believe an unmarried candidate is handicapped. The main thing people want to know is that the candidate can and will do a good job. Whether you are single, married, or divorced, someone will say your family or lack of family is a problem if you are a woman. Only widows seem to escape these myths. Forget the concern and package yourself as you are. Remember, the minute a woman runs for office, she is no longer a traditional woman—she's a role model, who, in the case of the personal and public in particular, cannot be the mirror image of the Political Man. She breaks the mold.

Even a few women running for office can make a big difference for all women. I have noticed that when a woman runs against a male incumbent, whether she wins or not, he invariably becomes more sensitive to women's issues. Even *speculation* about a particular woman running against a male incumbent is almost certain to produce an improvement in his performance on women's issues. It's amazing. Whether female candidates win or lose, the odds are they will improve women's status by running.

And the odds are also that if more people would vote, and vote smarter, women's concerns would be advanced and more women would be elected.

Voting Smarter

It's a shocking fact: A minority of the electorate wins elections in the United States—*not* a majority. The minority wins simply because the majority does not vote. Just as shocking, the United States ranks *last* among the world's top 20 major democracies in voter registration rates.[1] Millions of Americans throw away their votes—and their chance to be a part of the winning edge—at each election. On women's issues, only a relative handful of ballots are needed to swing almost any election and bring an end to women's political dilemma.

Do your part in changing this picture. If you are not registered to vote, call your local election agency now and find out how to register, or call the local office of one of the major organizations listed in the resource section. If you are registered, vote in both the primaries and general elections.

If you need convincing about the importance of your vote, read on.

Why People Do Not Vote

Many people do not vote because they believe a single vote does not count. In the past 25 years, two presidents—John F. Kennedy (1960) and Richard M. Nixon (1968)—won by only a few hundred thousand votes, a very small percentage of the voting population.[2] It has been said that if one more person per precinct nationwide had voted for Hubert H. Humphrey, he would have defeated Richard Nixon in 1968.

Since 1974 I have closely followed about a thousand races in which the outcome affected women's-rights issues. Here are just a few examples of what I have observed.

• In 1976, Senator Daniel Patrick Moynihan defeated leading feminist Representative Bella Abzug in the Democratic primary in New York by less than 10,000 votes out of over 916,000 cast; in 1980,

Republican Senator Alphonse D'Amato, outspoken right-to-lifer, defeated leading feminist Representative Elizabeth Holtzman in the general elections in New York by 1 percent of the vote (81,304 votes out of the nearly 6,000,000 cast). In both races there were more than two candidates and the other candidates took a large percentage of the votes from the women.

• In 1982, pro–women's-rights advocate State Senator Ruth McFarland (D) was defeated by right-wing Republican Representative Denny Smith (anti-ERA, anti-choice in abortion) in the Fifth Congressional District of Oregon by 2 percent of the vote, or some 4,954 votes (of 202,858 cast).

• In state legislative races, it is not unusual for a candidate to win by a few hundred votes. For example, in Anne Arundel County, Maryland, in 1982, Ann Irvine lost by 246 votes to right-to-lifer Bob Kramer in a multi-member district race.

• In statewide races in 1982, two governors—James Thompson (R-IL) and George Deukmejian (R-CA)—won by about 1 percent or less of the vote. Thompson won by about 5,000 votes out of approximately 3.6 million cast.

The presidential general elections attract the largest number of voters. Yet even in this highly publicized election, only a little more than half the electorate votes, while over 50 million people throw their votes away. Ronald Reagan was elected by 26.7 percent of the electorate in 1980. Fewer bother to vote in general elections held in even-numbered, nonpresidential years. Fewer still (25 percent) vote in the primaries of these years. And in the odd-numbered-year local or state elections, even less of the eligible population votes.

Who are America's nonvoters? Unfortunately, most are members of groups that tend to support women's rights: the young and the minorities; the unemployed; the service workers; and people with family incomes under $15,000.[3] These groups usually lag behind the general population in percent registered and even further behind in percent voting.

Many people don't vote because voting is still not easy. The United States is the only major democracy that puts the entire burden of registration on the voters themselves (in other countries, people are automatically registered when they reach voting age). Furthermore, registration rules vary from state to state. In some states, particularly in the Deep South, the creation of barriers to registration and voting has been a deliberate strategy to prevent black impact on elections. For example, in North Carolina there are 505,000 unregistered blacks whose votes could have defeated Senator Jesse Helms; he won his 1978 race by a margin of 102,000 votes. In South Carolina, where there are 292,000 unregistered black voters, Senator Strom Thurmond won by 70,000 votes.[4]

Although blacks, unquestionably, have been the most abused population in voting-rights denial, they have not been the only group of potential voters discouraged from exercising their rights. Young voters, 18–21 years old, also have been consistently underregistered (only 35 percent). Although registration in school has begun in some states to encourage their participation in elections, it is still not widespread.

Voting counts. That is why voting has been made more difficult for certain segments of the population, such as blacks in the South. The Voting Rights Act of 1964 and its extension in 1983 are critical in helping blacks obtain justice in voting. "Project Big Vote" is a major current civil-rights effort to increase black voter registration.

It's not just registration that discourages voting, but also the fact that elections are held on working days, and polls are open mostly during working hours. To make voting more accessible to wage earners, elections could be held on a Saturday or Sunday (as in some other countries), or election days could be designated national holidays, or workers could be given time off to vote.

Even the time of year has been used in some localities to discourage voting. Illinois primaries and Chicago city elections are still held sometime between mid-February to mid-March when the weather is often bitter-cold and snowy; thus did the infamous Chicago political machine ensure a low voter turnout. Scheduling particularly affects primary elections, whose dates differ from state to state, making them difficult for a transient population to remember.

The trend in state election laws over the past ten years has been to make voting more accessible and convenient for the voter. Twenty-one states and the District of Columbia now have mail registration procedures, and four states have some form of Election Day registration.

Voting Smarter Means Voting in Primaries

Although in many areas there are nonpartisan elections for positions like local school board memberships, most of the nation's electoral and governmental systems are based on political primaries. To ignore this is to discount your own political clout.

Independent Registration Means Less Voting Power

Twenty-three states require that a voter be registered as a Democrat or Republican in order to vote in the primaries for the nominees of one of the major parties.[5] Increasingly, however, many voters who are disenchanted by both major political parties have been proudly registering as "Independents."

It can be politically ineffective to be registered as an Independent. In some states, it amounts to throwing away an opportunity to exercise voting power by voting in the party primaries: Essentially, an Independent loses the chance to participate in the selection of the candidates of *either* party—and in many elections, winning the primary is tantamount to winning the election.

Let's face it—in much of the nation, one party tends to dominate elections at the local and state levels; thus, voting in the primary is voting in the election that decides who finally wins. Even most congressional seats and state legislative seats in the nation are safely in the hands of a single party. Not voting in the primaries for those "one-party" seats is simply throwing away the vote that counts.

So few people vote in primaries that it's obvious they view them as much less important than general elections. This could not be further from the truth. Primaries provide the major party choices for the general elections, and they can and do effectively eliminate popular choices. For example, because Republican primary voters are the more conservative members of their party, Republican party nominees are also frequently more conservative. With two-thirds of the electorate merely passive observers of perhaps the most critical stages of the political process—the candidate-selection process—both parties have essentially offered us the choices of only a minority of voters.

Beware of Independent Voting and Third-Party Choices

Although independent voting and third-party voting are becoming increasingly popular, the voter should be aware that he or she may unknowingly be aiding a "spoiler" strategy, where a candidate who cannot win is running in order to split the vote and thus cause another candidate to lose. Voting smarter means figuring out the effect a third-party or independent vote might have before making your choice.

In some general elections, independent and third-party voting can be effective in sending a political message of disapproval to the major parties. A third party can even become a major party, as the Republicans did in 1860 on a platform of the abolition of slavery. This, however, has been all too rare in American history, and voters should therefore be careful that the third-party or independent choice does not serve only to elect their *least* desirable choice. For example, John Anderson's 1980 presidential appeal siphoned votes from Carter, not from Reagan. In 17 states Anderson took enough votes from Carter to give Reagan a plurality of the popular vote and therefore all of the electoral votes from those 17 states.[6] Had this been a closer race, the Anderson votes alone would have defeated Carter, who was clearly the second choice of most Anderson voters.

Identifying the "Real McCoys": A Language and Performance Test

Everyone is for women's rights—or so every candidate would have you believe. Knowing how to tell the phonies from those who are sincere about supporting women's issues is one key to voting smarter.

Although every politician says he is in favor of women's rights, the phony candidates usually add a *"but."* They're for equal rights *but* not the amendment. They are for equal pay *but* against having too many governmental regulations, or against creating too much paper work in enforcing the regulations. (Can you imagine them declaring they are against paper work in stopping crime?) They are for women's right to choose abortion *but* against Medicaid funding of abortions for poor women. The *buts* go on and on, and they are the dead giveaway of a phony.

The grandstanding candidate also injects into the debate extraneous issues that are a fraud and a smoke screen. "I'm for affirmative action *but* not mandatory quotas." The truth is, no one is for mandatory quotas. "I'm for equal rights *but* not unisex toilets." Who cares about unisex toilets?—they are not the issue.

Phonies usually claim to agree with women's goals, but they differ with the advocates of the goals on the method or process for achieving them. "I'm all for equal rights, *but* I don't believe in tampering with [amending] the Constitution." Of course, these very same people are very willing to amend the Constitution to accomplish one of *their* goals, like abolishing legalized abortion.

Phonies tend to be patronizing: "I know you women are well intentioned, *but* you don't understand how insurance really works." The subject varies, but the theme is the same.

Phonies are always *personally* troubled by the issue: "I'm *personally* on your side, *but* . . ."

Sexist language in a candidate's speeches, public statements, responses to questionnaires, and campaign literature can be a big clue to the phony. A candidate genuinely sensitive to women as a voting constituency would avoid the gaffe committed by Senator Fritz Hollings (D-SC) with his early campaign brochure entitled *The Thinking Man's Dark Horse for '84.* After nearly 20 years of the women's movement, if the candidate is still using all *he*'s and no *she*'s, *men* instead of *women and men,* you can bet he hasn't really absorbed much on the hard-core issues either.

Candidate sincerity should also be measured by what they have done or are doing in public service. Their votes or views on issues are just one indicator. Others equally or more important: Do they provide leadership on the issue (as opposed to just a vote)? Do they initiate programs and solutions? Do they fight for the positions? Do they occupy a position of influence in the political arena on the issues?

Beware of candidates who tell you they have an "open mind" on issues that have been around for a long time. If they haven't yet formulated positions on the ERA, abortion, affirmative action, child care, etc., they shouldn't be running in the first place. To have an open mind on a new issue is understandable, but not on issues that have been kicked around in public debates. Such candidates may be dodging a commitment one way or the other in order to play to all sides. You have no guaranties where they'll land once elected to office.

In using language or performance tests to judge candidates, do not become a purist. People and campaigns make mistakes. A decision as important as whether or not to support a candidate should not rest on a mistake or two; it should be based on the candidate's *pattern* of behavior. Is this candidate generally and in important matters better than the opposition? A candidate could even be against your positions or beliefs in an important area but, overall, still be better than the opposition.

The seniority of an incumbent or his/her position of power, like a committee chair, should also be taken into consideration. Perhaps the incumbent is about equal to or not quite as good on issues as the opposition but occupies a key legislative position. Perhaps the committee chairperson, though not as good on the issues, can actually be more helpful on the issues because of his/her power position. Or perhaps the incumbent's reelection would block a far worse legislator next in line to take this powerful position. Real political choices are difficult, and simplistic notions can be dangerous.

Moreover, in politics, what is unsaid is often more important than what is said. Candidates frequently do not mention issues they deem controversial or "too hot" to handle. If candidates speak about your issues only before audiences agreeable to your viewpoint, it's fairly safe to assume they are weak supporters. If they never mention these issues or always avoid them, the odds are better yet. If candidates agree with only the more popular part of an issue, what about the other part?

Voting records are one of the most reliable indications of candidates' real positions on issues and are an absolute essential for evaluating a candidate running for the same office again or trying to move up in the political system.

Phonies on women's issues frequently blame their vote against women's rights on their wives, daughters, or secretaries. Now really! These men would be the last to consult these women before voting on other matters; but when they vote against women, they blame, of course, other women. When checked, women closest to the candidate are frequently found to be on the side of women's rights.

Phonies will also defend their votes on the basis of their constituencies' desires, knowing how hard it is to check the accuracy of this. But as we saw time and again with the ERA, even when we could produce objective public-opinion polls of legislators' districts, their votes did not change.

The best way to spot a phony is to contact the groups and organizations advocating a position of concern to you and ask about the candidate's record. These groups will gladly offer their recommendation. Candidates can fool some of the people, but not those who, day in and day out, are watching over the issues of importance to you.

An efficient means of acquiring this information is to join an organization that is politically aware and involved. Organizations send out newsletters and other literature in which candidates are evaluated on issues of concern. They also hold meetings attended by candidates where participants can ask questions.

With all this information, you may end up with more insight into a candidate than the candidate can survive.

Knowing the Team and the Players

Judging the candidates strictly as individuals is dangerous. Voting smarter means knowing the power relationships in the legislative bodies of this country. Committee chairs have enormous power—all bills have to go through the committee system in both houses of Congress and every state legislature. Contrary to popular myth, it isn't simply a choice between Tweedledee and Tweedledum—there are differences between the parties right now that are critical.

The party that is the majority in Congress, or the state legislatures, acquires all the power that goes with heading congressional and state legislative committees—positions that hold the power of life and death over bills. When moderates dominated the Republican party, this was not as critical. Right now, however, the Republican majority in the U.S. Senate means that key committees are headed by Senator Jesse Helms (R-NC), Senator Orrin Hatch (R-UT), and Senator Strom Thurmond (R-SC)—all of them hostile to women's-rights issues.

With hard-core Reaganites and New Right advocates in control of the GOP and initiating legislation designed to return women to the nineteenth century, control of congressional committees is crucial.

While the Democratic party has its "boll weevils" in its own conservative wing, Democratic control of Congress and most state legislatures is, for the present at least, less hazardous to women's interests. Yet some Democrats are injurious to women's issues. Knowing who belongs to which team is as essential as knowing which team player needs to be replaced. Voting smarter means knowing the teams and the players.

Postelection Watch

What happens after Election Day? How can voters monitor the performance of the elected candidates? Have the candidates who pledged to support your issues stuck with them when the chips were down and votes or action were needed?

Most major organizations, unions, and PACs monitor what happens after Election Day. Newsletters and other types of communications, such as telegrams and phone calls to the local leadership of the group, go to the members and supporters. These communiqués periodically report how their issues are faring and how the officeholders are performing.

There are disappointments. During the Equal Rights Amendment campaign, we learned the hard way that there are candidates who, once elected, do the opposite of what their campaigns promised. Fortunately, they are rare. Most officeholders perform pretty much as you would expect from their previous record, performance, and campaigning. The best way to make sure this happens, however, is to remain vigilant and to keep reminding them of the support for their campaign stand.

The first step in active citizenship is voting. The second is holding the candidate, once elected, accountable for his or her performance.

Like being an informed voter, this is not an easy task. That's why public-interest groups who monitor the various issues are so vital in a representative democracy. They serve to keep the media, supporters, and the public at large informed about what is going on with their particular issues.

Fortunately, women's groups vigorously monitor the progress of women's issues, and lobby regularly at national, state, and local levels on issues of the gender gap. Frequently we are joined by allies from other public-interest groups, such as Common Cause, senior-citizen groups, occupational associations with large female representations, trade unions, civil-rights and religious groups. Unfortunately, seldom, if ever, are we joined by business lobbyists or groups. Considering how numerous the latter are in state capitols and Washington, their absence of support is all the more remarkable.

Elections are a continuous process—no sooner is one over than the process begins again. When elections are viewed as a part of an ongoing process, the need for continuous vigilance becomes obvious. This is not new. As Thomas Jefferson said, "Eternal vigilance is the price of liberty."

Nor is the struggle for women's rights and recognition new. Nearly 100 years after Jefferson, the famed suffragist Susan B. Anthony wrote: "There shall never be another season of silence until women have the same rights men have on this green earth."

She also wrote: "There never will be complete equality until women themselves help to make laws and elect lawmakers."

The dream of the suffragists is about to be realized.

Appendix: Resource Guide

The following list of resources will help you become politically active. General political resources, key groups, and federal political action committees that support feminist women candidates and the issues they believe in are cited in alphabetical order under each category.

Unless otherwise stated, the materials are available at nominal cost and sometimes are free to members of the respective organizations. Remember to check at your local libraries also, both public and university. Although items like campaign manuals are not generally available, you may be able to persuade the librarian to order them. Manuals designed for candidates running for office are also excellent for running issue campaigns.

General Political Resources

Manuals and Training

Center for the American Woman and Politics
Eagleton Institute
Rutgers University
New Brunswick, NJ 08901

(201) 828-2210

The Center for the American Woman and Politics (CAWP) is a unique research, education, and public-service center established in 1971 at the Eagleton Institute of Politics at Rutgers University. It designs and sponsors a variety of programs aimed at developing and disseminating knowledge about women's political participation. A recent national forum for women state legislators is only one example. Many publications are available (cost varies), including a series of seven monographs that explore the routes of men and women into public office. Also available are reports from CAWP's program for women state legislators, "training manuals for women in government and politics," fact sheets providing current data on women in public office, and other CAWP project reports.

Democratic National Committee
1625 Massachusetts Avenue, N.W.
Washington, D.C. 20036

(202) 797-5900

The Democratic National Training Academy sponsors two-day workshops for candidates and campaigners at various times and in different parts of the country each year.

Party officials and political consultants provide the training on how to organize special constituencies (seniors, minorities, women), researching the opposition, communications skills, polling, fund-raising, phonebanks, targeting, etc. The usual charge is $125. Videotape training presentations on the following topics can be rented for $60 each or $195 a set: management; planning; budgeting; voter contact; targeting; media and communications; fund-raising; and direct mail. A videotape featuring Esther Peterson and U.S. Congressman Claude Pepper focuses on senior citizens (*Forget Not Old Friends,* $35). A campaign manager's manual covering topics provided in the academy sessions is available for $10. Other printed materials are available free of charge—issue papers for candidates, briefing papers on special constituencies, and a guide to consultants.

Federal Election Commission
1325 K Street, N.W.
Washington, D.C. 20463

(202) 523-4068
Toll-free (800) 424-9530
Call collect from Alaska or Hawaii (202) 523-4068

The Federal Election Commission is the government agency that implements the Federal Election Campaign Act of 1971. Free brochures on the following topics are available: contributions; candidate registration; volunteer activity; corporate/labor facilities; corporate/labor communications; independent expenditures; and political ads and solicitations. A monthly newsletter, the *Record,* reports on current rulings of the FEC and provides general information about PACs and related business. From the vast computerized records of the agency, one can order the campaign reports of candidates, PACs, and members of Congress. Training is provided at seminars throughout the country—call for details.

The National Women's Education Fund
1410 Q Street, N.W.
Washington, D.C. 20009

(202) 462-8606

The fund, founded in 1972, is a nonpartisan, national training and information service to assist women in gaining access to public policy positions. Political-skills workshops can be tailored for presentations to specific groups when requested. *The Campaign Workbook,* over 160 pages in the 1982 (third) edition, covers the nuts and bolts of how to run a political campaign: planning, targeting, polling, staff, voter contact, media, fund-raising. This new edition (price $25) has a section on judicial races and one especially for minority women. The following slide shows and films are available to rent or buy: a two-hour package designed to introduce women to politics, entitled *Making a Difference,* and three 20-minute packages on media, voter contact, and campaigning in general.

Project on Equal Education Rights (PEER)
1413 K Street, NW, 9th Floor
Washington, D.C. 20005

(202) 332-7337

PEER, a project of the NOW Legal Defense and Education Fund, promotes equal education in schools by advocacy in local communities. A new manual, *Organizing for*

Change ($12.95), is useful for organizing any issue campaign. It has chapters on targeting, analyzing goals, designing a plan, recruiting support, working effectively in groups and coalitions, using the media, budgeting and fund-raising. Also available from PEER are a 14-point public-policy agenda of actions to achieve educational equity and a candidate questionnaire to determine a candidate's commitment to equity in education.

Public Media Center
25 Scotland Street
San Francisco, Calif. 94133

(415) 434-1403

Running to Win is a comprehensive campaign manual originally produced for NARAL by Ann Beaudry in 1982, price $18. A 1983 edition has been published by the Public Media Center. In over 150 pages it covers strategy, planning, budgets, targeting, voter contact, media, fund-raising, volunteers, and candidate activity.

Republican National Committee
301 First Street, S.E.
Washington, D.C. 20003

(202) 484-6500

The RNC sponsors three-day workshops (some specifically for women) for local, state, and federal office candidates as well as campaign workers. Officials of the Reagan administration, party leaders, and consultants do the training on public-policy issues and campaign techniques (finance, voter contact, media, polling, etc.). The usual charge is $45. Currently the RNC is redesigning its campaign manual and other materials to be available in early 1984.

Voters for Choice
2000 P Street, N.W., Suite 301
Washington, D.C. 20036

(202) 659-2550

Voters for Choice is a nonpartisan political action committee formed in 1979 to elect legislators to Congress who are pro-choice on abortion. It supports candidates through contributions and through consulting services in such areas as fund-raising, issue management, and polling. *Winning with Choice: A Campaign Strategy Handbook* (1983, second edition, $35) is a candidate's guide to developing a pro-choice position, answering questions, knowing the opposition, etc. It includes case studies from the 1982 elections.

Women's Campaign Fund
1725 I Street, N.W., #515
Washington, D.C. 20006

(202) 296-5346

The WCF is a multipartisan political committee dedicated to helping feminist women candidates win elective office at all levels of government. It holds training seminars, provides technical assistance, and assists women in fund-raising from national PACs.

One two-day training session in 1983, for example, included all the nuts and bolts of campaigning, as well as meetings with congresswomen. Cost: $75.

Other General Resources

Almanac of American Politics, 1984
Government Research Corp., publisher
1730 M Street, N.W.
Washington, D.C. 20036

(202) 857-1400

This publication provides profiles of congressional districts, including census data and election results (incumbents' and presidential), and gives group ratings, key votes, publisher's ratings on liberal and conservative votes, campaign finance information, and brief biographies of all members of Congress. Also included are gubernatorial election results and brief biographies of sitting governors. Cost: $29.95 hardcover; $16.95 paperback.

America Votes
Congressional Quarterly, publisher
1414 22nd Street, N.W.
Washington, D.C. 20037

(202) 887-8500

Election results for all presidential, gubernatorial, and congressional races since 1945 are listed, plus county-by-county results for presidential elections. Published every two years; the 1983 edition has 1982 election data and costs $70.

Congressional Quarterly Editorial Research Reports
Congressional Quarterly, publisher
1414 22nd Street, N.W.
Washington, D.C. 20037

(202) 887-8500

CQ editorial research reports are available on virtually every current public-policy topic—the women's movement, energy, the environment, health, consumer protection, education, foreign policy, etc. About 15 titles are published annually in paperback, price range $7–12. A catalog is available free.

Congressional Quarterly Weekly Report
Congressional Quarterly, publisher
1414 22nd Street, N.W.
Washington, D.C. 20037

(202) 887-8500

The CQ *Weekly Report* (40 pages, average) provides comprehensive coverage of congressional action, Supreme Court rulings, and executive-branch action. Content of current issues and their political significance are reported, as are texts of presidential messages and press conferences, and the key votes of members of Congress. Subscription rates are quoted on request.

The Eleanor Smeal Report
Box 19995
Washington, D.C. 20037

(202) 337-0505

The Eleanor Smeal Report is an incisive source of information and analysis on women, their candidates and issues, and their effect on the American political scene. This twice-a-month report, mailed first class from Washington, provides concise commentary on emerging trends and the gender gap.

Federal Communications Commission
1919 M Street NW
Washington, D.C. 20554

(202) 857-1400

The Federal Communications Commission is the government agency that regulates interstate and international communications by radio, television, wire satellite and cable. FCC's free *Primer: The Law of Political Broadcasting and Cablecasting* deals with the law on broadcasts and cablecasts by candidates for public office, including equal time, censorship, reasonable access for candidates for federal office, the rates that may be charged candidates for time, the Fairness Doctrine and other information relevant to federal laws on political elections.

General Accounting Office
Document Handling and Information Services
P.O. Box 6015
Gaithersburg, Md. 20760

(202) 275-6241

The GAO is a government office that prepares studies and reports at the request of members of Congress and its committees. The focus of the GAO's work can be a particular government program, an agency, or an issue with legislation pending in the Congress. A monthly list of reports is available free, as are copies of the actual reports.

U.S. Government Printing Office
Superintendent of Documents
Washington, D.C. 20402

(202) 783-3238

A wealth of information is available from the U.S. government—literally thousands of books, periodicals, and reports. Begin by ordering the *Subject Bibliographies,* which lists more than 250 subjects. Check off the ones you are interested in—e.g., the U.S. budget, defense, child care, sanitation and sewage—and the documents office will send you bibliographies for those specific subjects. Materials are nominally priced and sometimes free.

Joint Center for Political Studies
1301 Pennsylvania Avenue, N.W., Suite 400
Washington, D.C. 20004

(202) 626-3500

The Center is a nonprofit institute that conducts research on issues related to blacks and promotes the involvement of blacks in government. It publishes a monthly newsletter, special reports, and current data on black voter registration.

National Journal
Government Research Corporation, publisher
1730 M Street, N.W.
Washington, D.C. 20036

(202) 857-1400

Available only by subscription, $455/year. Each weekly issue of the *Journal* (40 pages plus) has analytic articles on current political and governmental topics and trends, short notes on personalities, and full reports on major public-policy topics.

Politics in America
Congressional Quarterly, publisher
1414 22nd Street, N.W.
Washington, D.C. 20037

(202) 887-8620

The 1984 edition ($29.95) has lengthy biographies of members of Congress, including their legislative interests, successes or failures on specific bills, and an assessment of their effectiveness. It describes their strengths as candidates in general and "at home" in their districts or states. Demographic data on the home area as well as election statistics for the incumbent's seat and the presidential vote are given. Profiles of states include political, demographic, and economic trends for the state as a whole, major cities, and regions. Key votes, ratings of groups, special CQ ratings (party unity, liberal, conservative votes) and campaign finance information are reported.

Women's Research and Education Institute
204 Fourth Street, S.E.
Washington, D.C. 20003

(202) 546-1090

The institute was established in 1977 as an independent, nonprofit entity to bring together the work of researchers and policymakers affecting women. It is the nonpartisan research arm of the Congressional Caucus for Women's Issues in the U.S. Congress. Publications on the federal budget, employment, Social Security, older women, poverty, etc., are available at nominal cost. Conferences are sponsored periodically.

Key Organizations

American Association of University Women
2401 Virginia Avenue, N.W.
Washington, D.C. 20037

(202) 785-7700

The AAUW is a membership organization that supports equal education opportunities for women, career development, freedom of choice on abortion, and protection of the environment. It publishes the voting records of members of Congress and action alerts on key legislation. Materials on how to get voters out and how to get elected to office are available.

American Civil Liberties Union (ACLU)
132 West 43rd Street
New York, N.Y. 10036

(212) 944-9800

The American Civil Liberties Union, with 45 affiliates, works to protect the civil rights and civil liberties of all people through litigation, legislative lobbying, and public education. Women's-rights issues are among the ACLU's top priorities, with its National Women's Rights Project and Reproductive Freedom Project staffs litigating in these areas. ACLU attorneys provide assistance and advice to other attorneys on insurance discrimination, forced sterilization, Title VII, Title IX, etc. *Civil Liberties Alert,* the newsletter, reports the status of pending legislation, recommended action, and voting records of members of Congress. Free educational materials are available on a variety of issues. Two ACLU books, *Rights of Women* and *Rights of Gay People,* include pertinent state laws and regulations and list other resources.

American Federation of Teachers, AFL-CIO
11 Dupont Circle, N.W.
Washington, D.C. 20036

(202) 797-4400

The AFT of the AFL-CIO advocates the rights of its members (teachers and other professionals in education) through collective bargaining. It lobbies on both the national and local levels for measures that will improve education and the economic status of its members, the majority of whom are women.

American Nurses Association
1101 14th Street, N.W.
Washington, D.C. 20005

(202) 789-1800

The American Nurses Association is a federation of 52 state nurses' organizations, which are 97-percent female. The ANA promotes all issues related to the economic and professional status of nurses, including the ERA; pay equity; comparable worth; child care; discrimination in the military; and a multilateral, verifiable nuclear freeze. The association's periodic political-education workshops for members are open to the public.

B'nai B'rith Women
1640 Rhode Island Avenue, N.W.
Washington, D.C. 20036

(202) 857-6641

The B'nai B'rith Women work in their communities to combat anti-Semitism and to secure the rights of all. It provides leadership training for its volunteers and has many publications available, including *Women's World,* a monthly newsletter.

Catholics for a Free Choice
2008 17th Street, N.W.
Washington, D.C. 20009

(202) 638-1706

Catholics for a Free Choice was formed in 1974 to express its Catholic supporters'
pro-choice position on abortion. A series of booklets about abortion is available, as well
as special reports linking the issue with politics: *Abortion Politics and the American
Catholic Church* and *The Abortion Issue in the Political Process.*

Displaced Homemakers Network, Inc.
c/o Older Women's League
1325 G Street, N.W.
Washington, D.C. 20005

(202) 628-6767

The Displaced Homemakers Network concentrates on establishing employment and
training opportunities for displaced homemakers. It assists in the transition of homemakers to becoming wage earners and moving from dependency to economic self-
sufficiency. The network newsletter gives a legislative update on issues relevant to
displaced homemakers, including Social Security and pension reform.

EXPOSE, Ex-Partners of Servicemen (Women) for Equality
P.O. Box 11191
Alexandria, Va. 22312

(703) 370-3618

Ex-Partners of Servicemen (Women) for Equality, founded in 1980, has approximately 5,000 members in 50 chapters in the U.S. It works for legislation to protect
ex-spouses of military personnel by lobbying for military pensions, medical benefits, and
commissary and post-exchange privileges. EXPOSE works with lawyers to interpret
changes in laws pertaining to divorce, property, and child support. Local chapter
members work for changes in legislation, provide "friends in court" for women during
divorce proceedings, and monitor proceedings to pinpoint weaknesses in the system.
EXPOSE publishes a newsletter every two months.

Gay Rights National Lobby
P.O. Box 1892
Washington, D.C. 20013

(202) 546-1801

The Gay Rights National Lobby lobbies Congress for lesbian and gay issues and
against antigay issues and appointments. The lobby has a large constituent network and
maintains regional offices in San Francisco and Chicago. It works closely with women's-rights and civil-rights organizations on a broad range of social, economic, and
legal issues. One of its publications for candidates is *What If Your Constituents Ask?*

IMAGE
3219 Columbia Pike
Arlington, Va. 22204

(703) 892-0631

IMAGE is a national Hispanic civil-rights organization concerned with employment of Hispanics. This nonprofit organization works on legislative issues important to improving the status of Hispanics in the United States.

League of United Latin-American Citizens (LULAC)
400 First Street, N.W.
Washington, D.C. 20001

(202) 628-0717

The League of United Latin-American Citizens, which was founded in 1929 and has over 100,000 members in the U.S. and Puerto Rico, seeks full social, political, economic, and educational rights for Hispanics in the U.S. Among its programs of political advocacy on issues affecting Hispanics are those of HOPE (Hispanics Organized for Political Education), which works to awaken members' interest in national policy issues, and the National Women's Executive Committee, which seeks greater opportunities for women in the workplace and the community. LULAC's publications include the *LULAC News Tabloid, Latino* magazine, *Aviso Newsletter,* and the annual *HOPE Voter's Guide,* which gives congressional voting records on issues affecting Hispanics.

League of Women Voters
1730 M Street, N.W.
Washington, D.C. 20036

(202) 429-1965

The league is a nonpartisan organization for both men and women interested in the study of government. Training in the workings of government at all levels is available to members through local units of the league. Equality for women, as well as international relations, the environment—virtually all public issues—are of interest to the league. A variety of publications are available.

Mexican-American Women's National Association (MANA)
P.O. Box 2365
L'Enfant Plaza Station, S.W.
Washington, D.C. 20024

(202) 331-7667

MANA is a Hispanic feminist organization dedicated to achieving equal rights and opportunities for Chicanas in employment, housing, education, and other areas. A newsletter is available.

National Abortion Rights Action League
1424 K Street, N.W.
Washington, D.C. 20005

(202) 347-7774

NARAL, a membership organization with affiliates in 42 states, works to safeguard legal abortion. It provides training in lobbying and political activism and offers materials on reproductive rights, including current public-opinion data on abortion.

National Association of Commissions for Women
W.V. Capitol Complex
West Virginia 25305

(304) 348-8816

The National Association of Commissions for Women is an umbrella association for over 200 local and state commissions for women in the United States. The National Association advocates the appointment of women to policy positions in government and funding for women's programs, and is an exchange center for local and state commissions.

National Association of Social Workers
7981 Eastern Avenue
Silver Spring, Md. 20910

(301) 565-0333

The association has become increasingly active politically in response to cuts in social programs. A manual entitled *Power at the Polls,* on how to organize a voter-registration drive among the clients of social workers, is available for $3. Books on a variety of social-welfare issues are available also.

National Black Women's Political Leadership Caucus
2705 30th Street, N.E.
Washington, D.C. 20018

(202) 529-2806

The Caucus is a national membership organization that promotes the involvement of black women in politics. Issues training is provided through an annual legislative conference and a national convention.

National Coalition on Black Voter Participation, Inc.
"Operation Big Vote"
1301 Pennsylvania Avenue, Suite 400
Washington, D.C. 20004

(202) 626-3552

The National Coalition on Black Voter Participation, Inc., a nonprofit, membership organization, works through its "Operation Big Vote" to increase the level of voter-participation activities of all national black organizations and to develop autonomous local coalitions that conduct nonpartisan voter-participation campaigns. The National Coalition, consisting of over 85 organizations, serves the local coalitions with informational materials, technical assistance, training, and the free *Operation Big Vote* newsletter.

National Commission on Working Women (NCWW)
2000 P Street, NW, Suite 508
Washington, D.C. 20036

(202) 872-1782

The National Commission on Working Women, founded in 1977, is a private, non-profit organization which focuses on the economic status of nonprofessional women workers in clerical, sales, service and factory jobs. Its twenty-five-member Board has multi-sector representatives from corporations, unions, Congress, the media, academia and local communities. The Commission's areas of prime concern are wages and benefits, education and training, child and dependent care, self-esteem and dignity.

National Council of Jewish Women
15 East 26th Street
New York, N.Y. 10010

(212) 532-1740

The National Council of Jewish Women is a nonpartisan educational organization that focuses on helping women in their careers and addressing a broad spectrum of women's concerns. Organized in 1893, the NCJW has a membership of 100,000 in 200 affiliates. They play an advocacy role for women by testifying on legislation pertaining to day care, aging, the ERA, and other social and economic issues. Free publications are available on a variety of issues.

National Council of Negro Women
1819 H Street, N.W.
Washington, D.C. 20006

(202) 293-3902

The council is a coalition of church, women's, senior-citizen, and other organizations concerned with a variety of issues (housing discrimination, child care, employment, etc.).

National Education Association
1201 16th Street, N.W.
Washington, D.C. 20036

(202) 833-4000

The NEA's 1.7 million members promote the increased funding of education, high educational standards, and full human and civil rights. The association encourages political activism through education, lobbying, and (through its PACs) support of candidates.

National Federation of Business and Professional Women's Clubs, Inc.
2012 Massachusetts Avenue, N.W.
Washington, D.C. 20036

(202) 293-1100

The National Federation of Business and Professional Women's Clubs, Inc. (BPW/USA), founded in 1919, is the oldest and largest membership organization for working women in the United States. Its purpose is to promote full participation, equity, and economic self-sufficiency for working women. BPW/USA's bimonthly magazine, *National Business Woman,* and papers on legislative issues keep members in its 3,500 clubs (one in every congressional district) informed.

National Gay Rights Task Force
80 Fifth Avenue, Suite 1601
New York, N.Y. 10011

(212) 741-5800

The National Gay Rights Task Force, founded in 1973, is the oldest and largest
gay/lesbian membership organization in the U.S. The Task Force works on both
national and local levels to obtain civil-rights protection and equality of opportunity
for lesbians and gays. Serving as a resource and clearinghouse for local groups, the
organization works in coalition with other civil-rights and women's-rights organizations on AIDS, immigration, rape crisis centers, battered-spouse shelters, and other
issues. Publications on a wide range of topics are available.

National Lesbian Gay Democratic Clubs
1742 Massachusetts Avenue, S.E.
Washington, D.C. 20003

(202) 547-3104

The National Lesbian Gay Democratic Clubs, formed in 1982, acts as a link among
Lesbian Gay Democratic Clubs in the United States. The organization provides training for and works extensively on voter registration. It lobbies Congress on such issues
as funding for AIDS and adding sexual orientation to the protections of the Civil Rights
Act.

National Network of Asian & Pacific Women
3022 Q Street, N.W., Apt. A
Washington, D.C. 20007

(800) 638-8087

The National Network of Asian & Pacific Women, incorporated in 1982, represents
approximately 22 Asian and Pacific Island women's organizations. The network provides a resource-sharing center for Asian and Pacific Island women, develops leadership within these ethnic groups, and works to advance their national visibility. The
pro-ERA National Network encourages its members to become active politically and
works with other women's groups on health, education, social-welfare, and peace
issues.

National Organization for Women
425 13th Street, N.W.
Washington, D.C. 20004

(202) 347-2279

NOW was formed in 1966 to take action to bring women into the mainstream of
American life in full and equal partnership with men. With its over 250,000 members
and some 900 local chapters in all 50 states, NOW is the largest feminist organization.
Materials and training are available through NOW's Political Development Project.
Feminists who want to run for office are encouraged to call NOW's candidate hotline,
1-800-ERA-1984. Its monthly newsletter, the *National NOW Times,* and other publications cover feminist issues. At nominal cost, information is available on the Equal

Rights Amendment; reproductive rights; lesbian rights; and discrimination in insurance, credit, and the military draft.

National Women's Political Caucus
1411 K Street, N.W., Suite 1110
Washington, D.C. 20005

(202) 347-4456

The NWPC was founded in 1971 to increase the numbers of elected and appointed women at all levels of government. Training in campaign techniques is provided through its local affiliates and national conferences for its over 70,000 members and supporters. Its monthly newsletter, the *Women's Political Times,* and other publications cover current public-policy issues.

Nuclear Weapons Freeze Campaign
4144 Lindell Blvd., Suite 404
St. Louis, MO 63108

(314) 533-1169

The Nuclear Weapons Freeze Campaign is a national clearinghouse for local organizations and groups throughout the U.S. who support the freeze campaign movement. Its goal is to accomplish an immediate, bilateral (U.S.-Soviet Union) and verifiable freeze on the testing, production and deployment of all types of nuclear weapons and delivery systems. Focusing on electing a President and a Congress who support a freeze, the Freeze Campaign monitors Congressional votes on the issue in order to target national candidates. The monthly Freeze Newsletter disseminates information sent in by local freeze supporters to the several thousand local organizations in the U.S. and keeps them current on national arms legislation and other relevant information on the freeze issue.

Older Women's League
1325 G Street, N.W.
Washington, D.C. 20005

(202) 783-6686

OWL is a national membership organization that advocates policy changes in a variety of issues affecting midlife and older women—Social Security, health insurance, pension rights, employment, marital law, etc. Copies of testimony, position papers, and other materials are available.

Organization of Chinese-American Women
1525 O Street, N.W.
Washington, D.C. 20005

(202) 328-3185

The OCAW was created to promote equal participation of Chinese-American women in all aspects of American life. This membership organization provides training through conferences and materials on leadership, management and money dynamics, career fulfillment, educational equity, etc. It is active politically in monitoring legislation and public policy and supporting Chinese-American women who seek public office.

Planned Parenthood Federation of America
810 Seventh Avenue
New York, N.Y. 10019

(212) 541-7800

The federation supports family planning, birth control, and abortion rights through its numerous affiliates nationwide. It publishes a weekly newsletter that focuses on congressional activity. Other materials available include brochures on the current anti-abortion measures likely to come before the Congress and on Medicare funding for abortions.

Presbyterian Church (U.S.A.)
Committee on Women and the Church (COWAC)
The Interchurch Center
475 Riverside Drive
New York, N.Y. 10115

(212) 870-2019

The Committee on Women and the Church (COWAC) is the advocacy council for women's issues; it addresses problems women have in the church and society. COWAC supports the ERA and freedom of choice for abortion, and encourages the utilization of women's skills and expertise throughout the work of the church. A comprehensive list of its educational resource materials is available. A resource packet entitled *Women and Economic Justice* is available for $6.

Project VOTE
1200 15th Street, N.W., Suite 201
Washington, D.C. 20005

(202) 293-3933

Project VOTE is a nonpartisan organization that works through an informal coalition of labor, civil-rights, women's, church, community, environmental, and poor people's advocacy groups to increase electoral participation among low-income, minority, and unemployed citizens. Organized in 1982, Project VOTE engages in voter education and provides technical assistance in registering new voters, principally women waiting in lines to receive government benefits. It works for election reform to make registration easier and more effective.

Religious Coalition for Abortion Rights
100 Maryland Avenue, N.E.
Washington, D.C. 20002

(202) 543-7032

Thirty-one national religious organizations—Christian, Jewish, and others—support women's right to choose abortion through the Coalition and its local affiliates. A monthly newsletter is available, as is an "alert" system to stay up-to-the-minute on pending legislative action.

Rural American Women
1522 K Street, N.W.
Washington, D.C. 20005

(202) 785-4700

RAW is a nonprofit membership organization that shares information on agricul-
ture, health, employment, and the stability of rural communities. A 29-page report
entitled *How the Budget Cuts Undercut Rural Women* is available for $6. RAW's
newsletter updates the budget-cut issue periodically.

United Methodist Church
United Methodist Women
General Board of Global Ministries
475 Riverside Drive
New York, N.Y. 10115

(212) 870-3600

United Methodist Women (UMW) encourages its members to seek public-policy
changes of special benefit to women and children. Matters of racial justice, the ERA,
reproductive rights, and welfare rights are included. It provides training in political
skills to members and others; 50 such workshops will be held in 1984, with follow-up
training and support for women who want to run for public office.

Wider Opportunities for Women (WOW)
1325 G Street, N.W.
Washington, D.C. 20005

(202) 638-3143

Wider Opportunities for Women is a nonprofit network of 140 independent women's-
employment programs in 35 states. These programs provide direct services to approximately 250,000 women yearly in the area of job training and career counseling. WOW
works toward equal employment opportunities for women by reducing barriers in
employment, and works to affect public employment policy through advocacy and
education. It provides technical assistance in voter registration and get-out-the-vote
campaigns. *Connections,* WOW's quarterly network newsletter, focuses on employment issues.

Women in Communications, Inc.
P.O. Box 9561
Austin, Texas 78766

(512) 345-8922

WICI promotes the advancement of women in communications through its 12,000
members in some 90 chapters. Seminars and conferences promote professional development as well as political activism on issues such as the ERA and state statutes that
discriminate against women. A political manual, *Words into Action,* is available for $8.

Women's Equity Action League
805 15th Street, N.W., Suite 822
Washington, D.C. 20005

(202) 638-1961

WEAL is a national membership organization that, through research, public education, litigation, and legislative advocacy, focuses on the legal and economic rights of women. It offers a variety of publications on federal policies affecting women in such areas as the military, employment, insurance, and Social Security. Its monthly newsletter, *WEAL Washington Report,* covers legislative matters and is free to members; other publications are available at nominal cost.

Women USA
76 Beaver Street
New York, N.Y. 10005

(212) 422-1492

Women USA provides an informal communication network for women throughout the United States by keeping them up-to-date on relevant issues and activities including pending legislation, regulations, and important meetings and events. For periodic updates on women's issues and events, call the Women USA's hotline: (800) 212-4945 (For New York State only, call [212]344-2531.)

Women USA Fund, Inc.
11 Hanover Square
New York, N.Y. 10005

(212) 422-1913

Women USA Fund, Inc., is a nonpartisan, nonprofit organization that works with local coalitions formed around the issues of the gender gap, war and peace, economic equality, and social justice. In 1982 the fund ran pilot projects in six major states for voter registration and get-out-the-vote drives with potential women voters. Ten additional states are targeted for this action in 1984. The fund will publish a training manual on registration-drive techniques and how to mobilize the women's vote.

Women's International League for Peace and Freedom
1213 Race Street
Philadelphia, Pa. 19107

(215) 563-7110

The Women's International League for Peace and Freedom was formed in 1915 with the goals of eliminating barriers to world peace and eliminating racism, sexism, and economic exploitation. It has 130 local branches in the U.S. Training is provided in community organizing, polling, and voter registration. Its monthly magazine, *Peace and Freedom,* is free to members ($10 for others); legislative alerts are available (also $10); and a book on the federal budget and women, *Women, Taxes and Spending,* for $2.

Women's Strike for Peace (WSP)
145 South 13th Street
Philadelphia, Pa. 19107

(215) 923-0861

Women's Strike for Peace, founded 1961, is a national membership organization with local chapters that work for nuclear disarmament, substantive arms talks with the Soviets, and reduction of military buildup. *National Legislation Alert,* published monthly, is available with a $10 donation requested. It informs subscribers about pertinent legislation and events in the area of arms and peace issues and urges action to affect public policy.

Young Women's Christian Association of the U.S.A. (YWCA)
National Board
135 West 50th Street
New York, N.Y. 10020

(212) 621-5115

The YWCA has 2.5 million members in 400 chapters in the U.S. Among its priorities are the elimination of racism, the ratification of the ERA, equal pay for work of comparable value, improved child care, the reduction of teen pregnancy, and reduction of violence against all people. It cooperates with other groups in programs on campaign and political-skills training, get-out-the-vote efforts, and voter registration. The "Y" publishes a manual on voter registration entitled *Why Get Involved?*

Federal Political Action Committees

The PACs listed here (with name first; then description; sponsoring organization, if any; address; and a contact) all have one thing in common—they support *feminist* candidates. A brief description of the PAC's interest in the candidates is included here, but many PAC officials stated that exceptions to the prescribed criteria are sometimes made. You should remember that most of the organizations that are the sponsors of these national PACs have local affiliates and many of them have their own PACs for state and local races and sometimes for federal races, too. Most often, the national organization requires the approval of its local affiliate before it will endorse a candidate. The amounts reported here are total expenditures in the years indicated (if blank, the PAC is new). They should serve only to give you an idea of the level of activity of the PAC during that period—most have grown significantly.

ACTWU-PAC

The Amalgamated Clothing & Textile Workers Union PAC (ACTWU-PAC), whose membership is 65-percent female, endorses candidates whose voting records or positions support labor, civil rights, and consumer-related issues. Right-to-work, minimum wage, OSHA, child care, food stamps, the ERA, and equal pay are among the issues it focuses on.

Amalgamated Clothing & Textile Workers Union
815 16th Street, N.W.
Washington, D.C. 20006

(202) 628-0214   Liz Smith

1979–80 $183,000
1981–82 $231,000

American Academy of Physician Assistants PAC

The American Academy of Physician Assistants PAC concentrates its support on candidates who are on congressional committees that deal with issues affecting the physician assistants' profession or who are committed to taking a leadership role on these issues.

American Academy of Physician Assistants
1117 North 19th Street
Arlington, Va. 22209

(703) 525-4200   Robert Johnson

1979–80 $900
1981–82 $1500

American Dental Hygienists

The Dental Hygienists Association membership is 99-percent female. Its PAC seeks candidates who support preventive oral health care for all and improved economic status for women. It provides training to its members in the legislative process and in how to be effective politically.

American Dental Hygienists Association
444 North Michigan Avenue, Suite 3400
Chicago, Ill. 60611

(312) 440-8900   Julie Rosen

1979–80 $5,000
1981–82 $6,800

American Dietetic Association PAC

The Dietetic Association PAC seeks to influence the nomination or election to federal office of candidates who support maternal and child health, Medicare, Medicaid, nutrition education, and related matters. The association's membership is about 98 percent female.

American Dietetic Association
430 North Michigan Avenue
Chicago, Ill. 60611

(312) 280-5000   Michele Mathieu

1979–80   NA
1981–82 $19,400

American Federation of Government Employees PAC

The AFGE PAC is a liberal, pro-ERA national legislative organization. It principally supports candidates on the national level who have a liberal voting record or position on key federal employee issues. It seeks legislation for pay comparability for women, adequate health insurance and retirement programs, and other programs such as "flextime."

American Federation of Government Employees
1325 Massachusetts Avenue, Suite 501
Washington, D.C. 20005

(202) 737-8700   Betsy Reid

1979–80 $140,000
1981–82 $498,400

AFL-CIO COPE Political Contributions Committee

The AFL-CIO COPE Political Contributions Committee focuses primarily on economic issues. Key women's issues are included in the voting records the committee compiles and on which its support is based. Local endorsements are made at city, county, and state levels and backed, when feasible, by the national organization.

AFL-CIO
815 16th Street, N.W.
Washington, D.C. 20006

(202) 637-5000   Tom Donahue

1979–80 $1,197,000
1981–82 $1,180,000

American Federation of State, County & Municipal Employees (AFSCME) PEOPLE (Public Employees Organized to Promote Legislative Equality)

AFSCME's PEOPLE PAC uses criteria based on a broad range of bread-and-butter concerns to determine support of candidates. Its interests include key labor issues, Social Security, the ERA, Title XX, and food stamps. Prospective candidates should apply to the local and/or district council in the jurisdiction in which they are running.

AFSCME
1625 L Street, N.W.
Washington, D.C. 20036

(202) 429-1000   Girard Clark

1979–80 $249,000
1980–81 $224,300

American Federation of Teachers Committee on Political Education (AFT COPE)

The American Federation of Teachers Committee on Political Education is a legislative organization that concentrates on labor and educational issues. It supports candidates on the national level on the basis of endorsements made by unions in the local congressional districts or on the state level. Literature and information on candidates' voting records and pertinent issues are published for the membership.

American Federation of Teachers
11 Dupont Circle, N.W.
Washington, D.C. 20036

(202) 797-4436   Rachelle Horowitz

1979–80 $286,100
1981–82 $491,500

American School Food Service Association PAC

The American School Food Service Association was organized in 1982 for the single
purpose of protecting and promoting programs related to children's nutrition. The
association's PAC gives funding to candidates who support school lunch programs,
summer food service, nutrition training programs, child care, the Women and Infant
Care (WIC) programs, and related issues. There are local affiliates of the association
in every state.

American School Food Service Association
2757 N.E. 27th Avenue
Ft. Lauderdale, Fla. 33305

(305) 765-6248   Jane Wynn

1982   Organized

Americans for Democratic Action PAC

The PAC of the ADA, a liberal legislative organization, supports candidates who are
pro-ERA, pro-choice on abortion, and support social programs. An effort is made to
achieve some balance in race and sex among the candidates who receive PAC funds.
Local chapters must endorse the candidates also.

Americans for Democratic Action (ADA)
1411 K Street, N.W.
Washington, D.C. 20005

(202) 638-6447   Amy Isaacs

1979–80 $48,252
1981–82 $88,000

CWA-COPE Political Contributions Committee

The Communications Workers of America-COPE Political Action Committee focuses
its legislative activity on labor-related economic and social issues, of which women's-
rights issues are a part. Support is given to national candidates who have been endorsed
by the state and local unions.

Communication Workers of America
1925 K Street, N.W.
Washington, DC 20006

(202) 728-2300   Loretta Bowen

1979–80 $697,800
1981–82 $919,700

Flight PAC

The Association of Flight Attendants PAC (Flight PAC) generally follows AFL-CIO endorsement recommendations and supports candidates for office who are pro-aviation, pro-labor and pro–women's issues. Flight PAC, with an 85-percent female membership, represents 21,000 employees from 14 airlines. The organization monitors voting records, educates its members, and testifies on the federal level on the ERA; on age, marital, and pregnancy discrimination in employment, pension rights, and social welfare; and on aviation safety and other issues.

Association of Flight Attendants
1625 Massachusetts Avenue, N.W.
Washington, D.C. 20036

(202) 328-5400   Susan Bianchi Sand

1979–80   NA
1981–82 $1,500

Friends of Family Planning

Friends of Family Planning is a pro-choice PAC organized in 1979. It first contributed to congressional candidates in 1980–82. Its support for candidates is focused mainly in marginal races where choice is an issue.

Friends of Family Planning
122 Maryland Avenue, N.E.
Washington, D.C. 20002

(202) 543-7803   Henrietta Marshall

1979–80 $107,000
1981–82 $546,200

Human Rights Campaign Fund PAC

The Human Rights Campaign Fund PAC supports federal candidates in both primary and general elections who support civil rights for lesbians and gay men.

Human Rights Campaign Fund PAC
P.O. Box 1396
Washington, D.C. 20013

(202) 546-2025   Stephan R. Endean

1980 $ 1,000
1981–82 $ 144,642

Human Rights PAC

The Human Rights PAC supports candidates who are committed to a firm but even-handed human-rights policy in the U.S. and abroad, who take a leadership role in

promoting nonintervention and foreign aid, and who have a progressive record on
social issues. The PAC concentrates its support on candidates who face closely contested races on both the national and state levels.

Human Rights PAC
122 Maryland Avenue, N.E.
Washington, D.C. 20002

(202) 544-4666   William Goodfellow

Organized 1980 $3,978
1981–82 $45,784

ILGWU Campaign Committee

The ILGWU Campaign Committee endorses candidates who are dedicated to the
principles of the trade-union movement, the protection of civil rights, and the ratification of the ERA, and who have a strong commitment to social issues affecting the lives
of union members. It monitors legislation and publishes annual voting records on
issues. The Campaign Committee's sponsoring organization, the ILGWU, has 300,000
members, 85 percent of whom are women.

International Ladies Garment Workers Union
815 16th Street, N.W., Suite 103
Washington, D.C. 20006

(202) 347-7417   Evelyn Dubrow

1979–80 $ 925,000
1981–82 $1,150,000

NARAL PAC

Supports pro-choice candidates for U.S. House and Senate and some state legislative
races. The PAC is nonpartisan and flexible on other criteria. Gives in primaries as well
as general elections.

National Abortion Rights Action League
1424 K Street, N.W., 3rd Floor
Washington, D.C. 20005

(202) 347-7774   Marie Bass

1979–80 $369,000
1981–82 $558,500

National Association of Government Employees PAC

The National Association of Government Employees PAC supports candidates for
office who have a demonstrated record on or commitment to labor-related issues
affecting the status of public employees, which includes sex discrimination, federal
insurance programs, and day care.

National Association of Government Employees
2139 Wisconsin Avenue, N.W.
Washington, D.C. 20007

(202) 965-4411   Stanley Lyman

1979–80   NA
1981–82 $19,200

National Education Association PAC

The NEA PAC supports candidates who promote better education, increased funding for schools, and full human and civil rights.

National Education Association
1201 16th Street, N.W.
Washington, D.C. 20036

(202) 833-4000   Don Cameron

1979–80 $ 963,100
1981–82 $1,442,700

National Federation of Business and Professional Women's Clubs, Inc., PAC

The National Federation of Business and Professional Women's Clubs, Inc., PAC supports and funds candidates for national office in both primary and general elections who back the pro-working-women political-action goals of the BPW, including the ERA, day care, pay equity, elimination of insurance discrimination, etc. Thirty state PACs, using the same criteria, support and fund candidates on the state and local levels. PAC funds are available to subsidize political training for women who are potential candidates.

National Federation of Business and Professional Women's Clubs, Inc.
2012 Massachusetts Avenue, N.W.
Washington, D.C. 20036

(202) 293-1100   Irma Brosseau

1979–80 $40,300
1981–82 $99,100

NOW/PAC

NOW/PAC supports feminist candidates on the national level who support the goals of the National Organization for Women, including the ERA, reproductive rights, lesbian/gay rights, and economic equity for women.

National Organization for Women
425 13th Street, N.W.
Washington, D.C. 20044

(202) 347-2279   Judy Goldsmith

1979–80 $535,700
1981–82 $523,400

NOW/Equality/PAC

NOW/Equality/PAC supports candidates running for state or local office throughout the country who generally support the goals of the National Organization for Women, including the ERA, reproductive rights, lesbian/gay rights, and economic equity for women. Local issues are taken into consideration, and flexibility on criteria is deemed appropriate. State PACs that exist in 85 NOW units work closely with the NOW/Equality/PAC.

NOW
P.O. Box 317, 425 13th Street, N.W.
Washington, D.C. 20044

(202) 347-2279   Judy Goldsmith

1980–June 1983 $1,322,937

NWPC Campaign Support Committee

The Campaign Support Committee is one federal PAC of the National Women's Political Caucus (NWPC). It seeks candidates, especially women, who support the ERA, abortion rights, and other feminist issues. See also the Win with Women entry.

National Women's Political Caucus
1411 K Street, N.W., Suite 1110
Washington, D.C. 20005

(202) 347-4456   Gayle Melich

1979–80 $47,500
1981–82 $14,400

National Women's Political Caucus Victory Fund

The Victory Fund supports pro-women's-rights candidates on the state level. Pro-ERA candidates are emphasized.

National Women's Political Caucus Victory Fund
1411 K Street, N.W., Suite 1110
Washington, D.C. 20005

(202) 347-4456

1979–80 $800
1981–82 $143,800

Nuclear Freeze PAC (Freeze PAC)

Nuclear Freeze PAC is an independent PAC that supports candidates who espouse a rational arms-control policy (multilateral, verifiable, etc.) and have a progressive approach to politics. They are pro-ERA and do not support candidates who are anti–women's rights.

Nuclear Freeze PAC
1780 Broadway, Suite 1200
New York, N.Y. 10019

(212) 479-2566   Donald Spector

1979–80   NA
1981–82 $211

Political Action for Candidate Election for Human Services

Political Action for Candidate Election (PACE) supports candidates who are pro–
human services. Issues they have supported include funding for Medicaid/Medicare,
Social Security, abortion, the voting rights act, and the ERA. The 55 local PACE
affiliates are relatively autonomous in raising funds and endorsing candidates for local
and state office.

National Association of Social Workers
7981 Eastern Avenue
Silver Spring, Md. 20910

(301) 565-0333   Carol Scheffer-Hartmann

1979–80 $ 28,400
1981–82 $123,200

Nurses Coalition for Action in Politics (N-CAP)

The Nurses Coalition for Action in Politics (N-CAP) is the political fund-raising arm
of the American Nurses Association. Based on the state constituent organizations'
recommendations, N-CAP's board endorses candidates for national office who are
supportive of nursing issues and concerns and who generally espouse the resolutions
passed at ANA conventions. Thirty-three state PACs support state and local candidates.

Nurses Coalition for Action in Politics (N-CAP)
American Nurses Association
1101 14th Street, N.W.
Washington, D.C. 20005

(202) 789-1800   Kathleen Montgomery

1979–80 $ 99,679
1981–82 $190,619

Political Education for Nurses PAC (PEN PAC)

PEN PAC supports candidates who promote legislative and regulatory issues affecting
health-care delivery and who understand and work to expand the role of licensed
practical/vocational nurses (LP/VNs). PEN PAC testifies on both national and state
levels on issues related to pension discrimination, Social Security, Medicare and Medicaid reform, against budget cuts in health and education programs, and for programs
to elevate the status of LP/VNs.

National Federation of Licensed Practical Nurses
1110 Vermont Avenue, N.W., Suite 840
Washington, D.C. 20005

(202) 785-3200   Paul M. Tendler

1979–80 $ 8,100
1981–82 $ 8,000

Voters for Choice

A nonpartisan political action committee formed in 1979 to elect legislators to Congress
who are pro-choice on abortion. It supports candidates through contributions and
consulting services, including fund-raising, issue management, and polling.

Voters for Choice
2000 P Street, N.W., Suite 301
Washington, D.C. 20036

(202) 659-2550   Mildred Jeffrey

1979–80 $339,300
1981–82 $225,700

Win with Women

Win with Women is an NWPC PAC that supports candidates in federal and state races.
A primary objective has been supporting pro-ERA candidates, with emphasis on
women candidates.

National Women's Political Caucus
1411 K Street, N.W., Suite 1110
Washington, D.C. 20005

(202) 347-4456   Mia Homan

1978–82 $601,634

Women's Campaign Fund

The Women's Campaign Fund is a multipartisan political committee dedicated to
helping feminist women candidates win elective office at all levels of government.

Women's Campaign Fund
1725 I Street, N.W., Suite 515
Washington, D.C. 20006

(202) 296-5346   Stephanie Solene

1979–80 $708,400
1981–82 $596,800

Women For

Women For is an independent, feminist PAC working for the advancement of human and civil rights, better public education, peace, and the preservation of natural resources.

Women For
8913 West Olympic Boulevard
Beverly Hills, Calif. 90211

(213) 657-7411   Marilyn Kizziah

1979–80 $ 92,400
1981–82 $145,300

Notes

The Gender Gap: What It Is and What It Means to You

1. Postelection surveys and exit polls found a 5-percent gap overall, with women favoring the Democrats in 1982. This 5-percent gap reflects the average difference for CBS, ABC, NBC, and NES (National Election Studies) surveys. Both CBS and NBC reported a significant gap in over half the elections they studied. See Laurely K. Epstein and Susan J. Carroll, "Sex and the Vote: The 1982 Election Day Voter Polls" (Talk presented at the 1983 annual meeting of the American Political Science Association, Chicago) and Kathleen A. Frankovic, "The Gender Gap: 1982 and Beyond" (Paper presented at Conference on the Women's Vote in June 1983, convened by the League of Women Voters Education Fund). See also: Adam Clymer, "Women's Election Role Is Disturbing to G.O.P.," *New York Times,* 18 Nov. 1982, B19.

2. U.S. Department of Commerce, Bureau of the Census, *Current Population Reports,* Series p.20, no. 370, 3 April 1982, 3. Also U.S. Department of Commerce, Bureau of the Census, *U.S. Department of Commerce News,* no.CB83-63, 18 April 1983. League of Women Voters Education Fund, *Conference on the Women's Vote* (Washington, D.C., June 1983).

3. See for example Angus Campbell, Philip E. Converse, Warren E. Miller, and Donald Stokes, *The American Voter* (New York: John Wiley, 1960).

4. For a critique of the traditional literature on women and politics and a review of the current work, see Murray Goot and Elizabeth Reid, *Women and Voting Studies: Mindless Matrons or Sexist Scientism* (Beverly Hills: Sage, 1975); Bernice A. Carrol, "Review Essay: American Politics and Political Behavior, Part I," *Signs* 5 (1979), 289–306; and Virginia Sapiro, "When Are Interests Interesting? The Problem of Political Representation of Women," *American Political Science Review,* 75(1981), 701–16.

5. Audrey Siess Wells and Eleanor Cutri Smeal, "Women's Attitudes Toward Women in Politics: A Survey of Urban Registered Voters and Party Committeewomen," in Jane Jaquette, ed., *Women in Politics* (New York: John Wiley, 1974).

6. See for example "Opinion Roundup," *Public Opinion* (December/January 1983, 34–35), which documents, using ABC exit polls, a significant gap across education, income, and age categories. Also "Gender Gap Found in All Areas, Social Levels," *The Gallup Report,* no. 210, March 1983, 17.

7. Adam Clymer, *New York Times,* 18 Nov. 1982, B19.

8. G. Evans Witt, "Guest Outlook," *Opinion Outlook* (a service of *National Journal*), 9 March 1981. Witt is the director of polling for the Associated Press, Washington Bureau.

9. "Reagan Popularity—Men vs. Women," *The Gallup Report,* no. 210 (March 1983), p. 17, and Gallup Poll Survey Data, Interviewing Dates July 22–25, 1983.

10. David Garth, *The Garth Analysis*, September 1983, p. 8.

11. For more detailed academic discussions substantiating these basic points, see: Sandra Baxter and Marge Lansing, *Women and Politics: The Visible Majority* (Ann Arbor: University of Michigan Press, 1983); Ethel Klein, *Consciousness and Politics: The Rise of Contemporary Feminism* (forthcoming, Harvard University Press, 1984); Kathleen A. Frankovic, "Sex and Politics—New Alignments, Old Issues," *Political Science* 15 (Summer 1982): 439–48; Celinda C. Lake, "Guns, Butter, and Equality: The Women's Vote in 1980" (Paper presented at the 1982 Midwest Political Science Association, Milwaukee); Keith T. Poole and L. Harmon Ziegler, "Gender and Voting in the 1980 Presidential Election" (Paper presented at the 1982 annual meeting of the American Political Science Association, Denver); Arthur H. Miller and Oksana Malanchuk, "The Gender Gap in the 1982 Elections" (Paper presented at the 1982 annual conference of the American Association for Public Opinion Research); and Laurely K. Epstein and Susan J. Carroll, "Sex and the Vote: The 1982 Election Day Voter Polls" (Paper presented at the 1983 annual meeting of the American Political Science Association, Chicago).

12. See for example Adam Clymer's articles in the *New York Times,* "Women's Political Habits Show Sharp Change," 30 June 1982; "Doubt on Reagan Plan Spurred Voters, Polls Show," 8 Nov. 1982; and Howell Raines, "President Is Assailed by Women's Leader; 2nd Term is Opposed," *New York Times,* 10 July 1983; also, "Opinion Roundup," *Public Opinion* (April/May 1982, 27–32).

13. Aileen S. Kraditor, *The Ideas of the Woman Suffrage Movement 1890–1920* (New York: Anchor Books, Doubleday, 1965).

14. Louis Harris, "Their Newfound Clout Ends Benign Neglect" (Issue: Black Voters), *USA Today,* 19 May 1983, 11A.

15. See Baxter and Lansing; Klein.

16. Lucia Mouat, "Is There Really a 'Women's Vote'?" *Christian Science Monitor,* 24 October 1980.

17. Adam Clymer, "G.O.P. and ERA: Will It Matter?" *Los Angeles Herald Examiner,* 10 July 1980.

18. For a detailed analysis of the feminist vote from 1972 through 1980, see Klein.

19. Judy Mann, *Washington Post,* 16 Oct. 1981.

20. Frankovic.

21. Arthur Miller and Oksana Malanchuk.

22. "What Do Women Want?" *Newsweek,* 19 Sept. 1983. For a different focus see Klein.

23. Jack Carey "Women: Michigan's New Political Powerhouse" *Monthly Detroit.* January 1983, 48–51, 98.

24. "Gender Gap Found in All Areas, Social Levels," *The Gallup Report,* no. 210, March 1983, 13.

25. Raines.

Women's Rights and the Gender Gap

1. Academic studies that present analyses supporting the importance of equality issues include: Klein, Poole, and Ziegler, and Miller and Malanchuk.

2. American National Election Study (NES), 1980, conducted by the Center for Political Studies of the Institute for Social Research, the University of Michigan. The 1980 election study asked people to note the importance of a series of issues, including abortion, sex equality, defense spending, jobs, and busing. On a scale ranging from 0

(not important) to 100 (most important), the mean rating for women was statistically significantly higher than men's on both abortion (72 vs. 82) and sex equality (70 vs. 78). For further discussion of the greater saliency of women's-rights issues to women, see Poole and Ziegler and E. Klein.

3. NES, 1980.

4. NES, 1982.

5. Ibid. The correlation (r) between evaluations of the candidates on women's issues and the vote in 1982 shows a much stronger relationship among women:

	House	Senate	Gov.
Men	.20	.12	.18
Women	.30	.34	.29

6. NES. 1982.

7. Louis Harris & Associates, "The Business Week/Harris Poll," *Business Week*, August 1983, 93.

8. Louis Harris & Associates, *The Harris Survey*, New York, Tribune Company Syndicate, Inc. 12 August 1982.

9. "The 1980 Virginia Slims American Women's Opinion Poll," Roper Organization, Inc., 15. A majority of women today (53 percent) say that in 1980 women have achieved greater respect for themselves as individuals as compared to ten years ago. This represents an increase of 15 percent from a decade ago. A poll conducted by IWY Commission in 1975 found that the majority of women feel that women's lives have improved, in part because of the efforts of the women's movement. See also Keith T. Poole and L. Harmon Ziegler, "The Diffusion of Feminist Ideology," *Political Behavior* 3 (1981), 229–56.

10. See Joyce Gelb and Marian Lief Pallery, *Women and Public Policy* (Princeton: Princeton University Press, 1982); Joyce Gelb and Ethel Klein, *Women's Movements: Organizing for Change in the 1980s* (Washington, D.C.: American Political Science Association, 1983).

11. Eleanor Flexnor, *Century of Struggle* (Cambridge, MA: Harvard University Press, 1959).

12. For the historical significance of this visibility, see Klein.

13. *The Equal Rights Amendment: Guaranteeing Equal Rights for Women Under the Constitution* (Washington, D.C.: United States Commission on Civil Rights, Clearinghouse Publication 68, June 1981) 8.

14. Stanley K. Henshaw and Greg Martire, "Morality and Legality," *Family Planning Perspectives* 14 (March/April 1982), 54. Based on a poll commissioned by *Life* Magazine and conducted by Yankelovich, Skelly and White.

15. Deborah Jacobs and Susan Dickler, *Winning with Choice: A Campaign Strategy Handbook* (Washington, D.C.: Voters for Choice, 1982), "Literature Search on Public Attitudes about Abortion 1972–1981," conducted by Market Opinion Research, table 6c.

16. Ibid., table 6B.

17. Ibid. See also *The Garth Analysis,* September 1983, p. 16.

18. Christopher Tietze, *Testimony Before the Subcommittee on Health and the Environment of the House Committee on Energy and Commerce,* 28 June 1983, table 1.

19. Ibid., 19.

20. Louis Harris, "Big Shift in Single-Issue Voting Expected This Fall," *The Harris Survey* (New York: 11 March 1982), 2.

21. Louis Harris, "Big Shift . . . ," 3.

22. Samuel R. Berger, *Dollar Harvest* (Lexington, MA: Heath Lexington Books, 1971).

23. "ERA Spotlight Is on Florida," *St. Petersburg Times,* 7 June 1982, 18A.

24. Quoted from an April 15, 1982, letter to a constituent, Senator Warren Henderson (R, 25th District, Sarasota, Fla.).

25. A 1979 study of California driving performance by the California Department of Insurance shows that male drivers have 1.43 times as many reported accidents as females. Andre Maisonpierre, vice-president of the Alliance of American Insurers, submitted a statement at the hearing on H.R. 100, Nondiscrimination in Insurance Act, 20 May 1981, at 202.

26. GEICO mailing signed by John J. Byrne, CLU, Chairman of the Board, regarding the "Volume-Benefit" term life-insurance plan. Rates were to be guaranteed until 17 June 1983.

26. Phoenix Mutual Life (Connecticut), "1/1/83 Non-Smoker Dividend Scale Per $1000-Variable Policy Loan Rate," 1983 *Best's Flitcraft Compend,* 446.

27. An example can be found in *Best's Flitcraft Compend* (A. M. Best, 1982), 331 and 333.

28. G. H. Miller, Ph.D., and Dean R. Gerstein, Ph.D., "The Life Expectancy of Non-Smoking Men and Women," Department of Health and Human Services, *Public Health Reports,* July/August 1983.

29. U.S. Congressman John R. Dingell, "Statement on H.R. 100," Non-Discrimination in Insurance Act hearing before the Subcommittee on Commerce, Transportation, and Tourism, 20 May 1981, at 27.

30. Price Gaines, ed., *1981 Time Saver for Health Insurance,* National Underwriter Company (Cincinnati). State Farm Mutual (Bloomington, Illinois) Hospital Surgical Policy Plan 3 at age 30–34, premiums for males are $266.50 and for females $552.50, excluding pregnancy and childbirth, p. 122. Disability Allstate Life (Northbrook, Illinois) Disability Policy Class 4 at age 35 premiums for males are $225.50 and for females $575.40, excluding pregnancy, childbirth, miscarriage, and abortion (but including nonelective cesarean section), p. 5.

31. "Days Lost from Work Due to Job Injury, 1971–1972," National Center for Health Statistics, U.S. Department of Health, Education, and Welfare.

32. Louis Harris & Associates, "The Business Week/Harris Poll," 93.

33. Ibid.,

34. Julia Kagan, "Survey: Work in the 1980's and 1990's," *Working Woman,* August 1983, p. 24. Based on a poll conducted by Public Agenda Foundation headed by Daniel Yankelovich.

35. Ibid.

36. Donna Fenn, "Families: Day-Care Chains," *Working Woman,* August 1983, p. 104.

Economic Survival and the Gender Gap

1. Miller and Malanchuk.

2. See Louis Harris, *Testimony Before the House Select Committee on Aging* (14 June 1983) and Jeff Alderman, *The '82 Elections* (New York: ABC News Poll, interview date 2 Nov. 1983, Survey #0065).

3. See Louis Harris. Also *The Garth Analysis,* October 1982, December 1982, and May 1983.

4. Alderman, *The '82 Elections;* NBC News and the Associated Press, *Decision 82: General Election Results* (Findings of 14 separate Election Day voter polls conducted on 2 Nov. 1982). *The Garth Analysis,* October 1982.

5. Ibid.

6. "Reagan Economic Package," *The Gallup Report,* no. 194, Nov. 1981, 5. See also *The Garth Analysis,* May 1983.

7. Adam Clymer, "Women's Votes Are a Reagan Woe," *New York Times,* 19 Nov. 1981.

8. In 1982, according to the NES survey, women with less than a high-school education were more likely to disapprove of Reagan's handling of inflation (68 percent) and unemployment (79 percent) than were those with more than a high-school education (44 percent on inflation; 67 percent on unemployment), *but* higher-educated women are significantly more disapproving than educated men of Reagan's handling of inflation (an 18 percent gap) and unemployment (9 percent gap). Female heads of households are more likely to favor increased government involvement in getting people jobs (33 percent vs. 20 percent), while male heads of households look toward decreased government effort (51 percent of male heads of households want decreased effort, compared to 31 percent of female heads of households—a 20-percent gap). Female heads of households are also more likely to want an increase in government services (34 percent as compared to 20 percent of male heads of households), while male heads are more likely to seek further cutbacks in services (45 percent vs. 22 percent of female heads want cutbacks—a 23-percent gap).

9. "Final Carter Budget Sets Challenge for Reagan," *Congressional Quarterly Almanac* (1981) 276. These percentages are fiscal year 1982 estimates.

10. Sara E. Rix and Anne J. Stone, *Reductions and Realities: How the Federal Budget Affects Women* (Washington, D.C.: Women's Research and Education Institute, 1983), 11.

11. "Fiscal 1984 Budget," *Congressional Quarterly Weekly Report,* 5 Feb. 1983, 250–51.

12. Marion Anderson, *Neither Jobs nor Security* (Lansing, MI: Employment Research Associates, 1982), 1.

13. *Inequality of Sacrifice: The Impact of the Reagan Budget on Women* (Washington, D.C.: Coalition on Women and the Budget, 6 May 1982 and 16 March 1983).

14. Sara E. Rix and Anne J. Stone, *Impact on Women of the Administration's Proposed Budget* (Washington, D.C.: Research and Education Institute, Apr. 1982) 4, table A-2.

15. *Inequality of Sacrifice* (6 May 1982), 9.

16. These percentages are based on budget figures appearing in *Congressional Quarterly Almanac* (1981), 274–75; *Congressional Quarterly Weekly Report* (13 Feb. 1982), 230–31; *Congressional Quarterly Weekly Report* (5 Feb. 1983), 250–51.

17. Rix and Stone, *Reductions and Realities . . . ,* 18.

18. Rix and Stone, *Impact on Women . . . ,* 14.

19. Ibid., 15.

20. Ibid., 16.

21. *Inequality of Sacrifice . . . ,* 16 March 1983, 59.

22. Gloria Peterson Green and Rosalie K. Epstein, eds., *Employment and Earnings,* vol. 30, no. 7 (Washington, D.C.: Department of Labor, Bureau of Labor Statistics, July 1983), 9.

23. Michael A. Urquhart and Marilyn A. Hewson, "Unemployment continued to rise in 1982 as recession deepened" *Monthly Labor Review,* Feb., 1983, p. 150.

24. Ibid., 149.

25. Ibid., 151.

26. See NES, 1982. Also *The Garth Analysis,* May 1983.

27. NES, 1982.

28. Jeffrey D. Alderman, *ABC News/Washington Post Poll,* July 1983.

War, Violence, and the Gender Gap

1. "Opinion Roundup," *Public Opinion* (April/May 1982), 27–32. See also Frankovic.

2. *The Gallup Report,* June 1981, 29.

3. Louis Harris, *Testimony Before the House Select Committee on Aging,* 14 June 1983.

4. Ibid.

5. For a full development of this argument, see the *amicus curiae* brief of the National Organization for Women, *Rostker v. Goldberg,* Sup. Ct., March 1981, October Term, 1980, no. 80–251.

6. *The Gallup Report,* June 1981.

7. Sandra Baxter and Marjorie Lansing, *Women and Politics* (Ann Arbor: University of Michigan Press, 1983), 58.

8. *The Garth Analysis,* July 1983.

9. "A WEAL Kit: Women in the Military" Weal Facts, Women and Combat," (1980 Women and Military hearings, at 56. (Washington, D.C.: Women's Equity Action League, 1982), p. 2.

10. Hoyt Gimlin, editor, *The Women's Movement: Agenda for the '80s,* Marc Leepson, "Women in the Military" Washington, D.C.: Editorial Research Reports, Congressional Quarterly, 1981, 83.

11. Ibid.

12. See the *amicus curiae* brief of the National Organization for Women, *Rostker v. Goldberg,* Sup. Ct. March 1981, October Term, 1980, no. 80–251, 6.

13. *Recruitment Statistics and Policies Pertaining to Women in the Active Armed Services* (Washington, D.C.: Women's Equity Action League, January 1983), 3.

14. See *amicus curiae* . . . , 6.

15. Shirley Robson, "Women in Combat" film of the Everywoman television series, produced by Evening News Association, September 1978.

16. Gimlin.

17. Ibid., 84.

18. "Women in the Army," *USA Today,* 14 July 1983, 9A.

19. *The Gallup Report,* April 1981, 7.

20. "Private Violence: Child Abuse, Wife Beating, Rape," *Time,* 5 Sept. 1983, 18.

21. *The Gallup Report,* April 1981, 8, see also Nov. 1982, 6.

22. *Time,* 5 Sept. 1983, 18.

23. *Fact Sheet on Family Violence* (Washington, D.C.: Center for Women Policy Studies, June 1983).

24. Ibid.

25. "Congress Reconsiders Legislation to Fund Shelters," *Response to Violence in the Family and Sexual Assault* 6 (July/August 1983), 1.

26. "Congress to Reconsider Domestic Violence Legislation," *Response to Violence in the Family and Sexual Assault* 6 (March/April 1983), 3.

The Promise Broken by Republicans

1. George Gilder, *Wealth and Poverty* (New York: Basic Books, 1981).
2. Ibid., 130.
3. Juan Williams, "Reagan Offers Defense on Rights Record," *Washington Post,* 2 Aug. 1983, A-1. Also Steven R. Weisman, "Reagan Strongly Defends Policies on Minority and Women's Rights," *New York Times,* 2 Aug. 1983, A-1. Text of the remarks by the president to the American Bar Association, 1 Aug. 1983. The White House, Office of the Press Secretary.
4. Louis Harris, *Testimony Before the House Select Committee on Aging,* 14 June 1983.
5. Fred Barbash, "Administration Defies Women in Bias Funds Case," *Washington Post,* 6 Aug. 1983, A-2.
6. Felicity Barringer, "Congressional Group's Brief Disputes Justice Sex-Bias Stand," *Washington Post,* 9 Aug. 1983, A-2.
7. Rex E. Lee, *A Lawyer Looks at the Equal Rights Amendment,* (Provo: University of Utah Press, 1980).
8. Don Rothberg, "Reagan On Totally Different Track than GOP," *Associated Press,* March 1982.
9. "Getting a Gender Message," *Time,* 25 July 1983, 13.

The Party Dilemma: What Real Choice for Women?

1. The Senate vote was taken 28 June 1983.
2. Judy Mann, *Washington Post,* October 31, 1980, B.A.
3. Lenore Weitzman, "Economics of Divorce: Social and Economic Consequences of Property, Alimony and Child Support Awards," 28 *UCLA Law Review,* 1181-1981, p. 1251.
4. These figures are derived from 1982 votes of state legislators on ERA ratification in the Florida, Illinois, North Carolina and Oklahoma legislatures. I conducted an analysis of the 1982 ERA legislative votes; it was released to the press by the National Organization for Women, June 24, 1982.
5. Center for the American Woman and Politics, "Women Officeholders Speak on Women's Issues" (New Brunswick, N.J.: Rutgers University). Information in this flyer was taken from "Profile of Women Holding Office II" in *Women in Public Office: A Biographical Directory and Statistical Analysis, 2d ed.,* compiled by the Center for the American Woman and Politics (Metuchen, N.J.: Scarecrow Press, 1978).
6. Ibid., "Women and Men Holding Office."
7. David B. Truman, *The Governmental Process* (New York: Alfred A. Knopf, 1960), 100.
8. Ibid. Truman references for this information: Herring, *Group Representation Before Congress* (Baltimore: The Johns Hopkins Press, 1929), 186.
9. Frances Lear, "Why Would a Democratic Woman Go to the Polls?," *Washington Post,* 7 July 1983, A 25.

PAC Women: Fund-Raising for Campaign Dollars

1. See the Resource Guide for FEC listing. See also Edward Roeder, *PACs Americana* (Washington, D.C.: Sunshine Services, 1982).
2. *Buckley v. Valeo,* 424 U.S. 1 (1976)

3. For a thorough discussion, see Elizabeth Drew, *Politics and Money: The New Road to Corruption* (New York: Macmillan, 1983).

4. "Corporate Woman: Career Women Push for More Clout in Politics," *Business Week,* 1 Nov. 1982, 83.

5. Ibid.

6. For further discussion of the controversy around PACs and campaign financing, see Tom Watson, "Soaring Campaign Spending Generates Renewed Interest in Election Finance Changes," *Congressional Quarterly,* 16 July 1983, 1451. See also Alan Ehrenhalt, "Campaign 'Reform' No Boon to Challengers," *Congressional Quarterly,* 11 June 1983, 1191.

7. An example of a report of this campaign in Common Cause, *Money, Power and Politics in the 97th Congress,* 1981.

8. "Voter Distrust of PACs is Growing," *The Harris Survey,* no. 41, 23 May 1983.

9. If the donation of the item is to a PAC fund-raiser, it constitutes a contribution to a PAC and may be subject to PAC reporting regulations.

10. Ann E. Beaudry with Bob Schaeffer, *Planning to Win: State Legislative Campaigns* (Washington, D.C.: National Abortion Rights Action League Political Action Committee, 1982), 16–25.

Women on the Ballot—And in Office

1. Wells and Smeal, "Women's Attitudes Toward Women in Politics: A Survey of Urban Registered Voters and Party Committeewomen" (Paper presented at the 1972 annual meeting of the American Political Science Association, Washington, D.C., Sept. 5–9), 4.

2. Ibid., 7–8.

3. "The 1980 Virginia Slims American Women's Opinion Poll," Roper Organization, Inc., 37.

4. "Special Report: Behind the Gender Gap," *The Garth Analysis,* Sept. 1983, 18–19. See also the Roxanne Conlin race as reported in *Opinion Outlook,* 1 July 1982, 7.

5. Center for the American Woman and Politics, "Women and Men Holding Office," fact sheet taken from 1978 study, *Women in Public Office.*

6. The Rev. Jesse Jackson, president of Operation PUSH, has been delivering this same message, especially to blacks and minorities, in 1983.

7. Center for the American Woman and Politics, "Are Political Women Ambitious? Yes!" fact sheet taken from 1978 study, *Women in Public Office.*

8. Susan J. Carroll and Wendy S. Strimling, *Women: Routes to Elective Office: A Comparison with Men's* (New Brunswick, N.J.: Rutgers University Center for the American Woman and Politics, Eagleton Institute of Politics, 1983).

9. Center for the American Woman and Politics, "Women and Men Holding Office," fact sheet taken from 1978 study.

10. Ibid.

11. Carroll and Strimling.

12. National Women's Education Fund, *Campaign Workbook* (Washington, D.C.: National Women's Education Fund, 1978).

Voting Smarter

1. Joshua Fischman, "Democracy Defamed," *Psychology Today* (Aug. 1983), 8.

2. In 1960 Kennedy won by 118,550 votes, and in 1968 Nixon won by 510,314 votes,

as cited in *The World Almanac and Book of Facts 1983* (New York: Newspaper Enterprise Association, 1983), 297.

3. U.S. Bureau of the Census, Current Population Reports, Series P-20, no. 370, *Voting and Registration in the Election of 1980,* U.S. Government Printing Office, Washington, D.C., 1982, 3.

4. "Jackson Voter Registration Drive: A Danger to Reaganism," *Human Events,* XLIII, 35 (27 Aug. 1983), 1.

5. *The Book of the States 1982–1983,* vol. 24 (Lexington, Ky.: The Council of State Governments), 110.

6. Based on Federal Election Commission state breakdown of 86.5 million popular-vote total. The 17 states were:

Arkansas	Massachusetts	Rhode Island
Connecticut	Michigan	South Carolina
Delaware	Minnesota	Tennessee
Hawaii	Mississippi	Vermont
Kentucky	New York	Wisconsin
Maryland	North Carolina	

Acknowledgments

Over my last dozen years of women's-rights involvement, my work has been largely a part of a team effort. This book is no exception.

More directly this book is a product of a team of three—Kathy Bonk, Toni Carabillo, and myself—with the support of several advisers and associates.

The book is the vision of Kathy Bonk, former media director of NOW's Equal Rights Campaign and Toni Carabillo, coeditor with Judith Meuli of the *National NOW Times.* Bonk believed the book, for us, was the next step to clarify the issues of the gender gap and to build an understanding of the women's vote; Carabillo was convinced a book by those of us who have actually participated in the evolution of issues and strategies and done the day-to-day organizing of the movement's campaigns was long overdue. Both believe in the power of the written word in organizing a political movement.

The demands of the movement for women's rights do not stand still for a book. Thus, we wrote this book in too little time, while we also participated in the on-going women's-rights events of the day. I kept saying we cannot write this book because there is no time to do it and participate in the upcoming elections; my associates kept taking the next step in the work. The book is both enhanced and limited by our constant activity for women's equality. But there is no question that this intense activity, along with our extensive backgrounds and research, offers a unique perspective.

The book is written as a Call to Action—an organizing tool for 1984 and future elections.

Carabillo, Bonk, and I have been working together on women's rights activities for over a decade. Bonk and I began working together in 1971 in Pittsburgh on a media reform project. Today Bonk is the leading expert on sex discrimination in the media. Bonk is some 14 years my junior and brings to our work a post-sixties generation perspective.

Carabillo, our senior partner, brings the experience of some 16 years of national women's-rights leadership. Carabillo and I have been working in the women's movement and writing together for better than 10 years. Carabillo was also the work's final editor before it was presented to Harper & Row editor Harriet Rubin. Rubin brought a supportive layperson's perspective to the work.

The work is the product of all of us. In the final analysis I take full responsibility, but acknowledge gratefully and with admiration their essential roles in its publication.

The book was written in the high-tech world in which both Carabillo and Bonk are comfortable. In the early days I used to write with Carabillo, exchanging copy between her Los Angeles home and mine on the East Coast via mail. Today we are writing via *electronic mail,* made possible by personal computers, word processing, and modems. Though Bonk and Carabillo have learned the system, I am still writing with a pencil. Fortunately, I had an able electronic translator and assistant Kathy Combes, who worked incredibly long hours entering data and copy into the computer and transmitting and receiving coast-to-coast. Without Combes's skills nights and weekends, there would also have been no book.

Many others assisted in the project. First, Charlie Smeal, my husband and partner, who kept us going, edited, transmitted data, and did anything and everything. Katie Harris, an associate and long-time women's-rights activist, assembled the Resource Guide with the assistance of Betty Feldman.

Ethel Klein, assistant professor of government at Harvard University, provided assistance in interpreting and analyzing polling data and in assembling research for footnotes in the first four chapters. She reviewed all data in those chapters, checked their statistical accuracy and significance, and wrote the footnotes concerning polling data for these chapters.

Judy Goldsmith, president of NOW, took time out of her impossible schedule to lend expertise and writing skills, especially for the second chapter. For the past several years, as officers of NOW, Goldsmith and I have worked together on many writing projects. Her editing skills greatly enhanced the insurance section of this book.

Bill Adler, our literary agent, provided encouragement and advice.

Finally, many colleagues and friends read sections of this book and provided sage advice and/or encouragement: Roger Craver, Molly Yard, Alice Cohan, Marion Wagner, Louis Harris, Thomas Hart, Lena Zezulin, and Judith Meuli, who, as I recall, was the first to insist the focus of the book should be the gender gap.

The gender gap, we believe, puts us at the threshold, at last, of organizing so that women *count* politically and can no longer be ignored.

To all who have helped make this happen, to all who dream of and work for women's equality, to those who gave of themselves so generously in the ERA Countdown Campaign, to the millions who support the ERA, and to all the organizations that work to realize the dream, but especially to the members of the National Organization for Women, I dedicate this book.